a Journey into the Human Body

Everyday Science Vol. 1

a Journey into the Human Body

Copyright © 2005 Sam & Youngin Singapore Pte Ltd.

World rights reserved. No part of this publication may be stored in a retrieval system, transmitted, or reproduced in any way, including but not limited to photocopy, photograph, magnetic, or other record, without the prior agreement and written permission of the publisher.

ISBN: 981-05-2242-8

Printed in the Republic of Korea.

How to contact us

E-mail: feedback@youngjin.com.sg

Address: Youngin Singapore Pte Ltd.
2F, 82 Amoy Street,
Singapore 069901

Telephone: +65-6327-1161
Fax: +65-6327-1151

Manager: Suzie Lee
Acquisition and Developmental Editor: Cris Lee
Copyeditor : Elisabeth Beller
Proofreaders : Elisabeth Beller, Yonie Overton

Story: Soo Oh
Art: Seok Yoon
Color: Winsorblue

Book Designer: Litmus
Cover Designer: Namu & Litmus

a Journey into the Human Body

Everyday Science Vol. 1

sam
Story | Soo Oh
Art | Seok Yoon
Color | Winsorblue

To Teachers and Parents

A Journey into the Human Body

There have long been reference books that show the human body and the internal organs, but we are confident that there has not been supplementary study material like this that teaches about the human body with interesting stories.

The Shadow Demon suddenly appears in a magic school, but he is challenged and flees into the body of the dormitory dean. To catch him, the headmaster calls upon brave children as volunteers. Riding in a pumpkin vessel, the children travel throughout the body and learn about many of its mysteries.

An unusual creature, Ken, acts as a travel guide to help the children explore and understand the human body. Readers are introduced to the functions of the internal organs of the human body through Ken's intriguing descriptions.

A Journey into the Human Body consists of twelve chapters. At the end of each chapter there are additional explanations of the organs that have been introduced.

Following the children's adventures with the bones, stomach, small

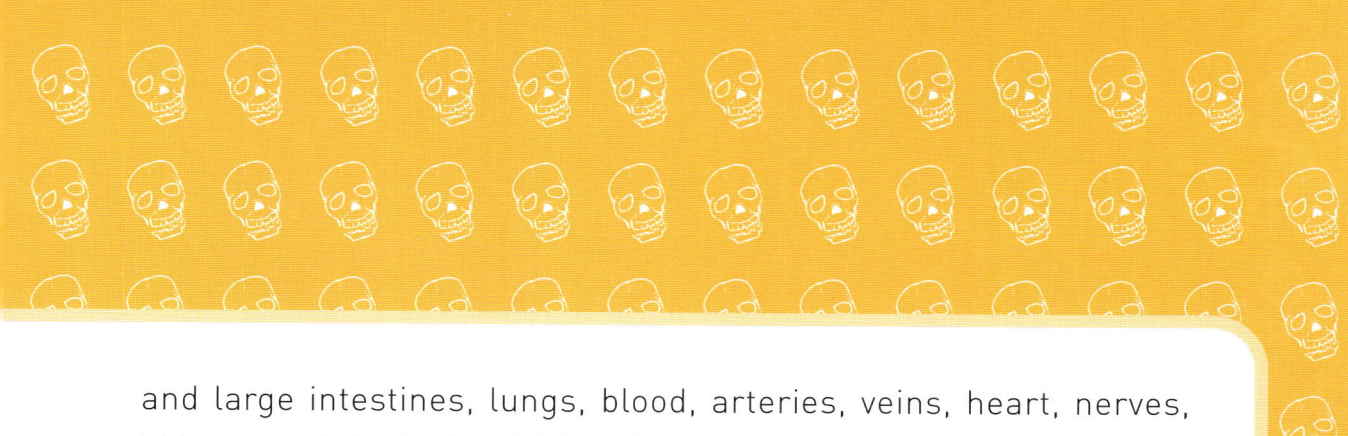

and large intestines, lungs, blood, arteries, veins, heart, nerves, kidneys, and the brain, children learn the structures and functions of each organ.

With this one book, children can acquire basic knowledge about the internal organs of the human body and additionally can learn some interesting facts.

What Are Educational Manga?

Educational manga can be children's favorite way to study fields that they find most difficult. We hope to relieve some of the burden of study while supporting learning. This is a new area that has garnered extremely positive response in Asia and has already become an established area of children's books. Children all over the world are very familiar with comics and often favor them over other media. We can make full use of the advantages of comics by creating exciting stories and attractive characters to awaken children's interests and affinities and to help them learn naturally. We hope many children will be able to expand their horizons through educational manga in libraries as well as at home.

Contents

Going into the Body — 8

Bone — 32

The Stomach — 52

The Small Intestine — 64

The Large Intestine — 72

The Lungs — 82

A Journey into the Human Body

96	The Blood
116	Veins and Arteries
124	The Heart
152	The Kidneys
168	The Brain
183	Going Home

Going into the Body

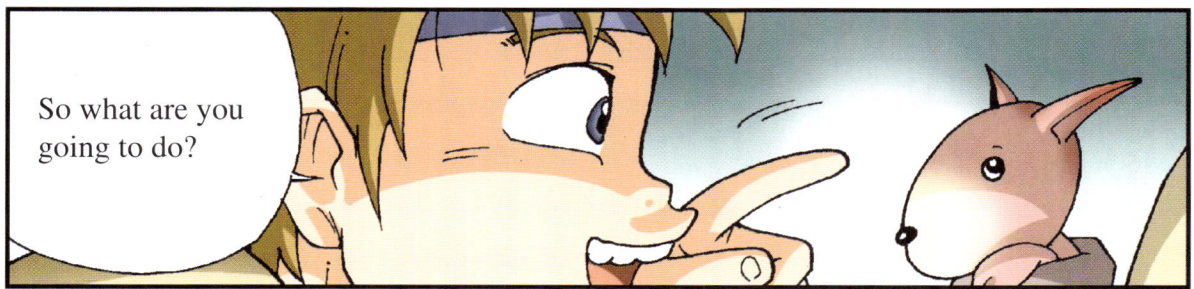

Going into the Body 11

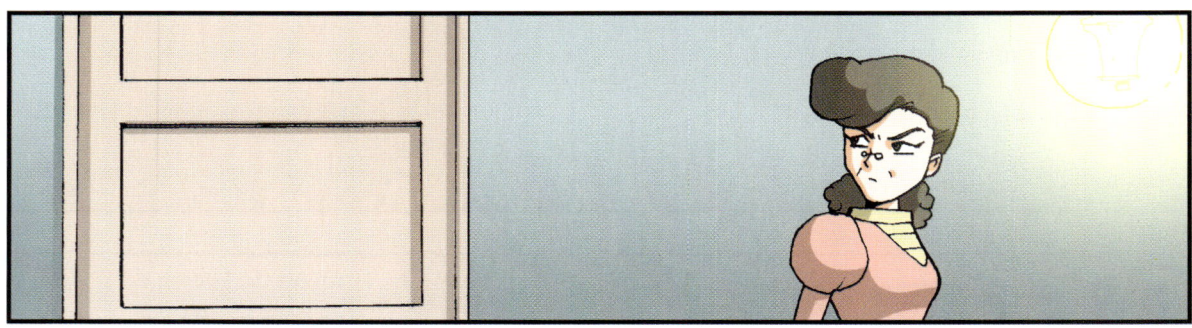

I don't hear any footsteps. I think they heard us.

No, please, no. If I get caught again I'll be expelled.

Going into the Body 13

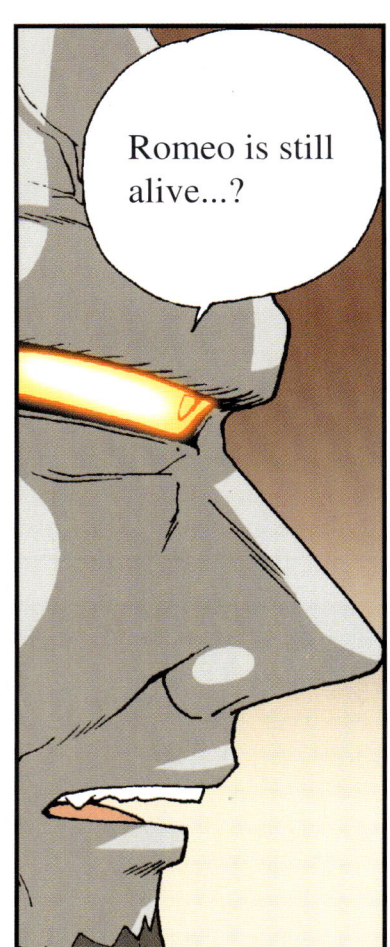

Ms. Forster is inhaling the Shadow Demon...

No, the demon is taking over her body.

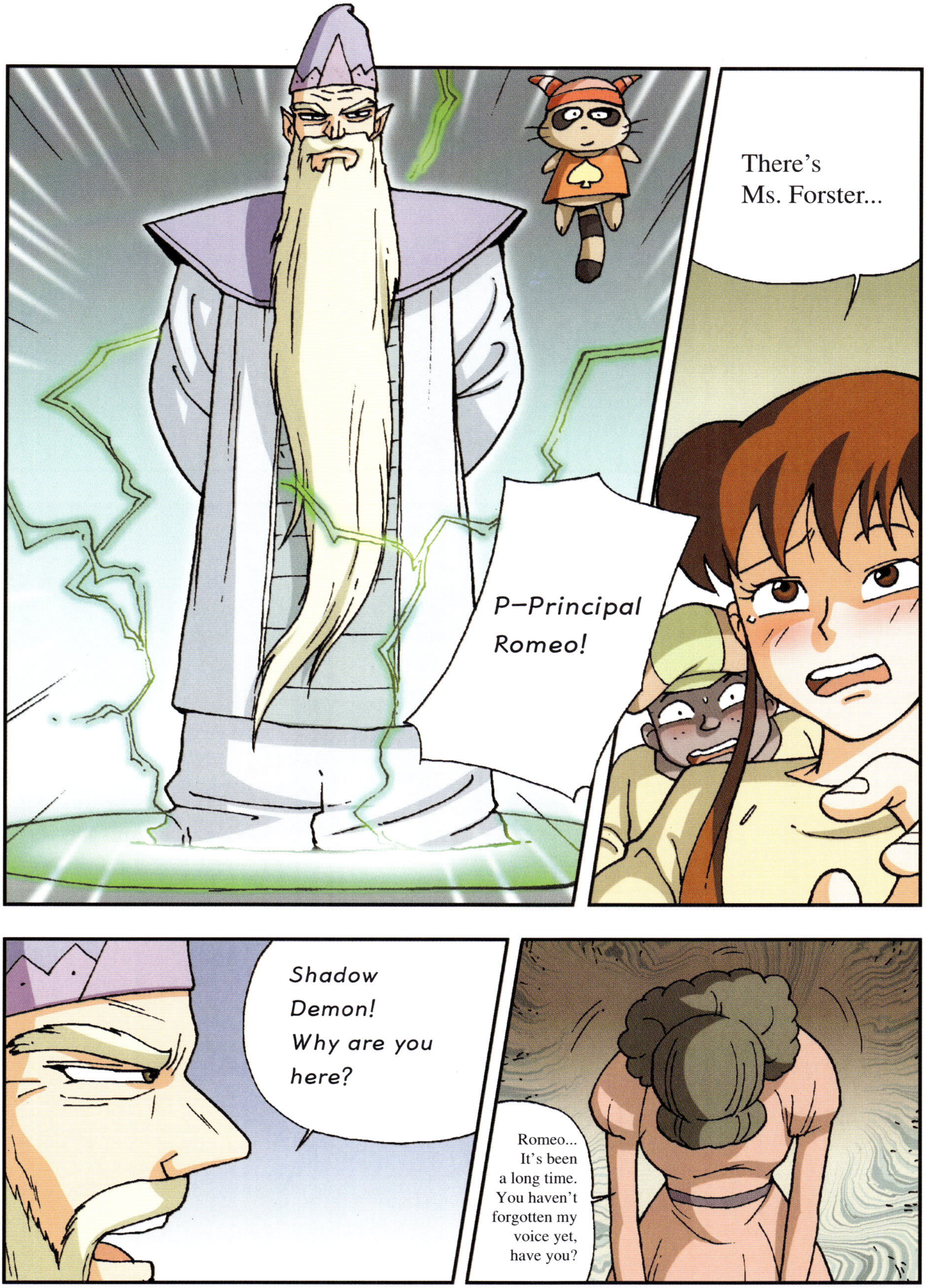

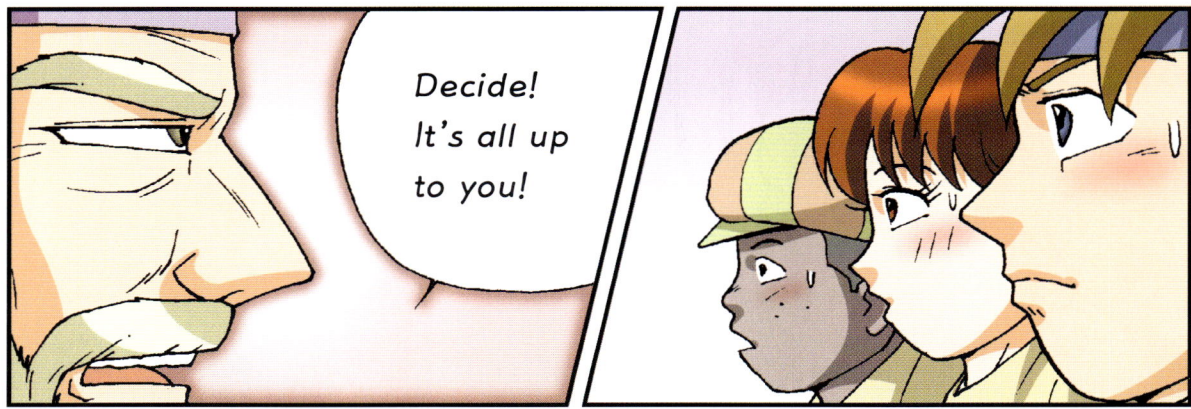

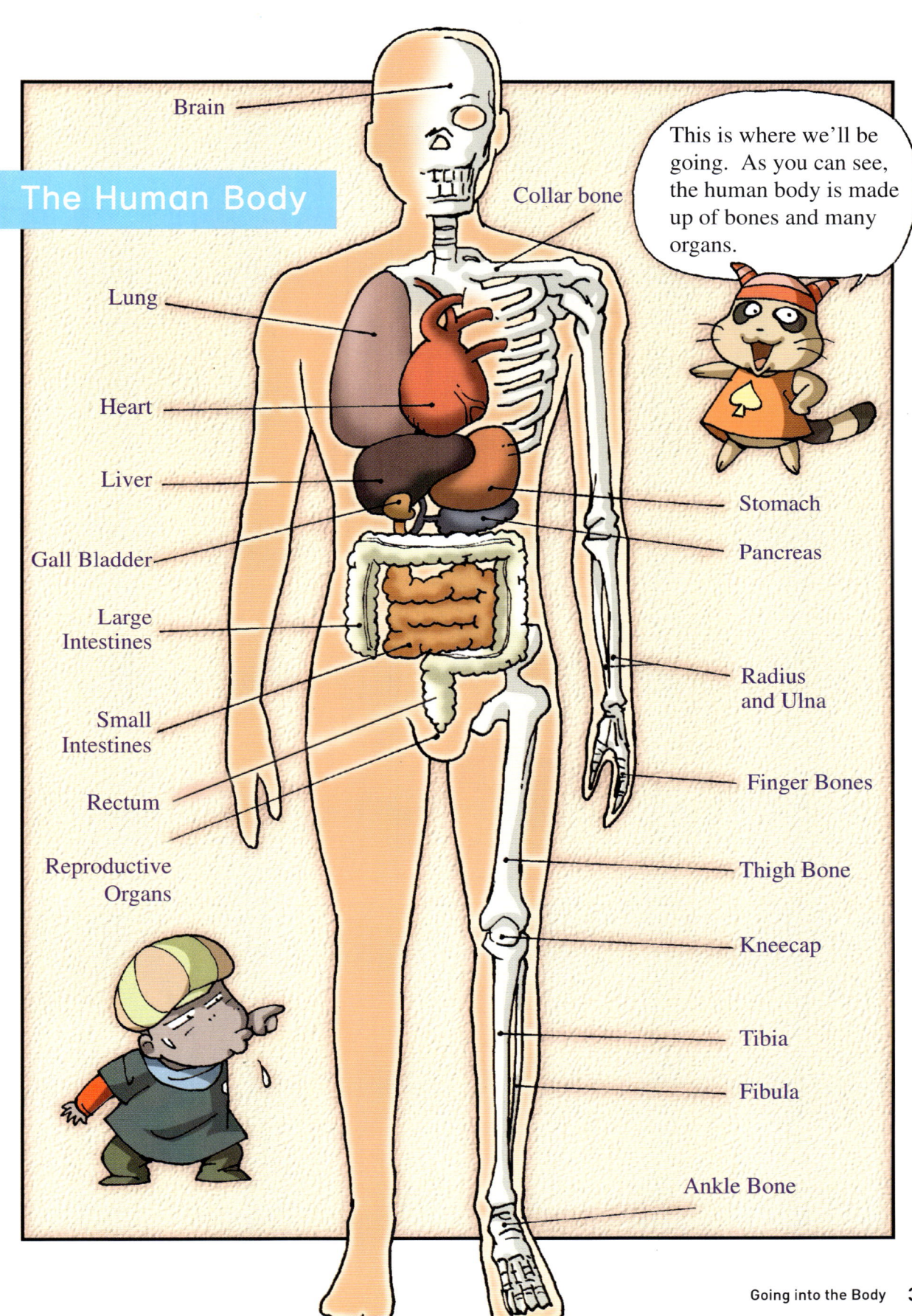

Bone

34   A Journey into the Human Body

Ken is very smart and knows a great deal about everything.

That's why we call him the "walking encyclopedia."

He'll be of great help to you on your adventure.

That wasn't such a great introduction, but we'll leave it at that for now.

It's time to go.

Whoa... We're going in!

Bone 35

ZOOM

……

The inside of the nostril is like an enormous cave.

It's so dark…

Principal Romeo, judging by the way the demon is controlling Ms. Forster, couldn't it be that it has entered her brain?

You'll find out once you inspect the brain.	But before that, you'll need a lot of knowledge about the body.

The best place to start learning the basics of the human body would be the bones.

That's why I'm here!

I know everything about all the bones in the world.

How can we learn about bones while we're in here?

Huh...??!!

"One of you call the skeleton. Hurry..."

"Call the skeleton..."

"...so I can demonstrate, and you can get it through your heads."

"Your magic skills couldn't possibly be so pathetic..."

"...that you can't even make a skeleton appear? If so, this fight is over!"

"We don't have a chance against the Shadow Demon!!"

"Ken! Calm down! None of us are that pathetic!"

38 A Journey into the Human Body

"I'll call the skeleton."

"A student of magic always carries around the bone of a chicken at least."

"Well then, shall we begin?"

"Hmm..."

Maxilla... Scapula...

Ulna...

Bone

Vertebra!

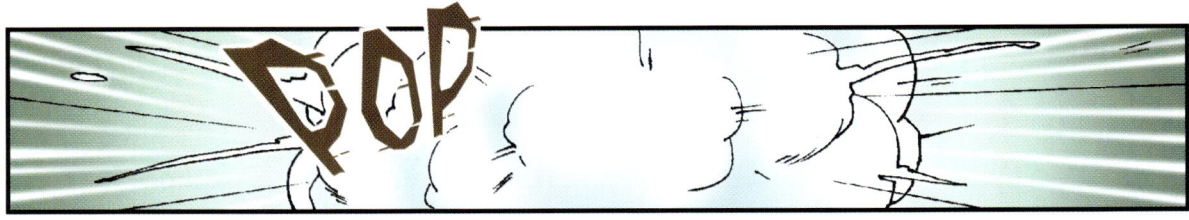

POP

It seems you have the basics down.

Let's see if you're as talented as you say you are.

All right. I'll start explaining, so listen carefully.

40   A Journey into the Human Body

There are 206 bones in the human body.

If the body were a house, the bones would be the pillars.

They support the body and protect the major organs.

Each bone has a unique function depending on its location and shape.

For example, the skull's job is to protect the brain inside it.

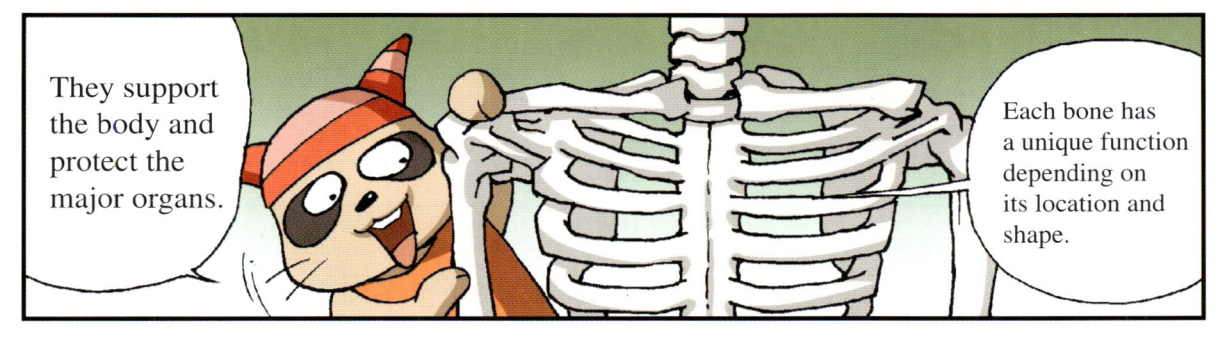

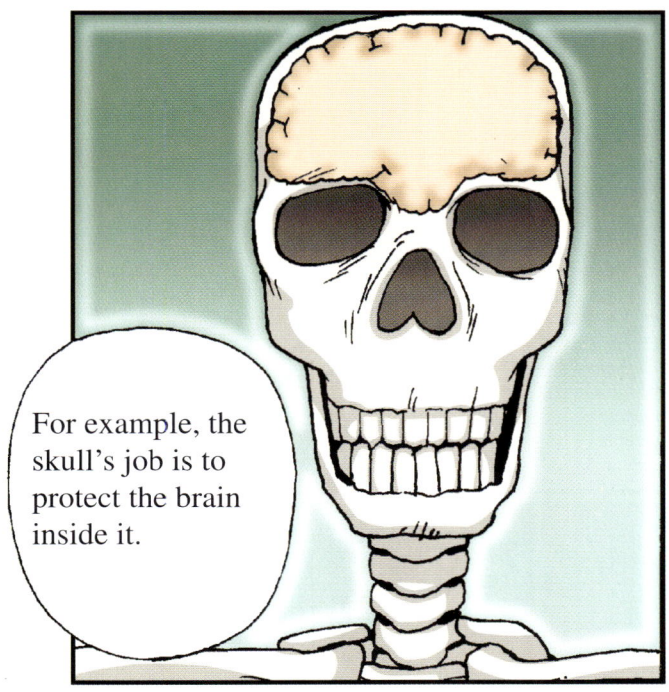

These arm bones make movement possible.

Look carefully.

Bone 41

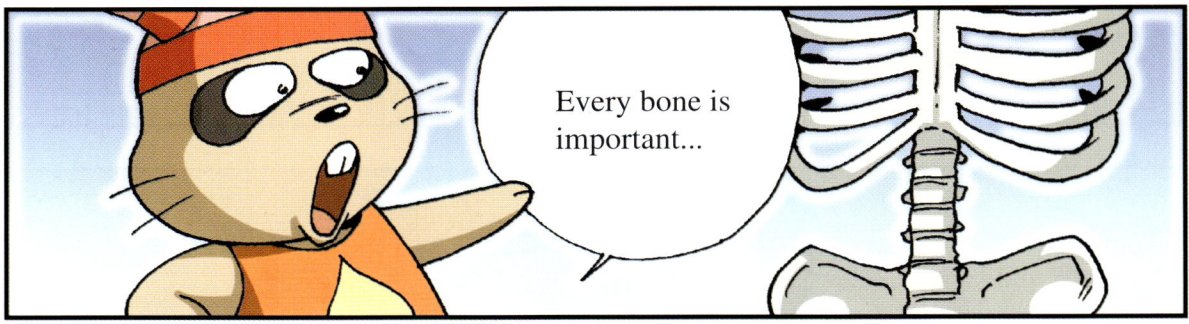

Wow! He's really smart!

He sounds like a professor!

Ahem...

Every bone is important...

...but the most important of all is the spinal column, which holds up the human body.

Whoa... I don't understand a word of what you're saying!

He's really an expert.

Just remember that the spine is made up of movable segments.

Each vertebra is connected by cartilage, allowing us to flex and bend our backs.

That's true!

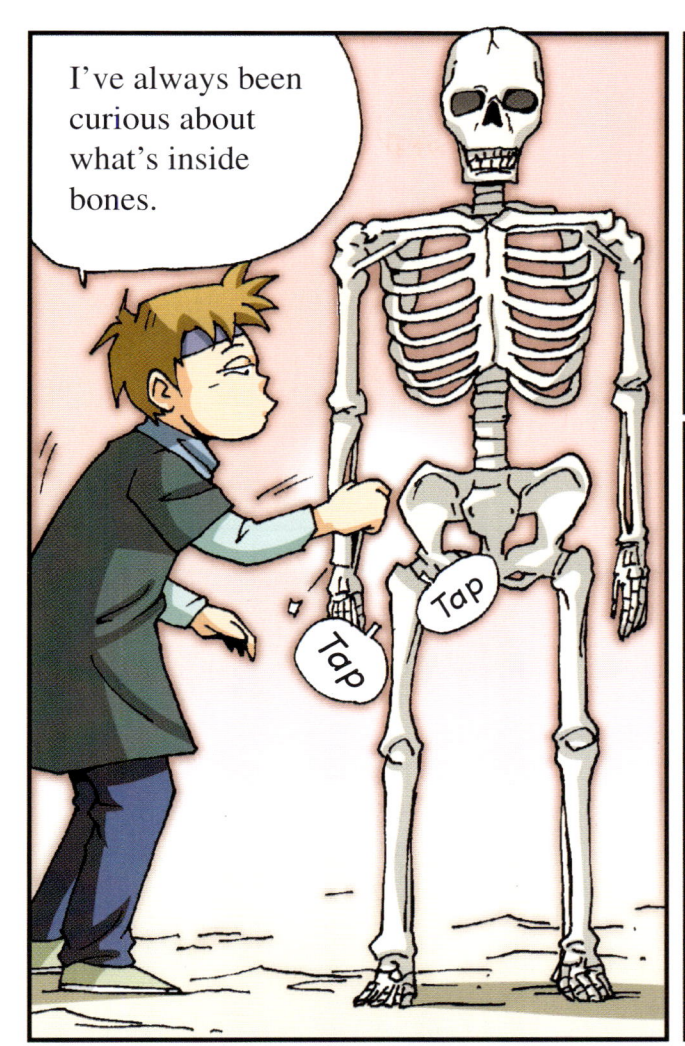

I've always been curious about what's inside bones.

Tap Tap

Don't poke at it like that!

Owww! Uh...What happened...!!

Right... I forgot...

It thinks you're trying to attack.

The skeleton will attack automatically if touched...

Bone 43

"Are you okay?"

"Be careful. The skeleton can be dangerous if you make it angry."

"All right. I'll keep that in mind."

"I've seen many wizards injured by the skeletons they summon."

"Want to use this magnifying glass that reveals everything? It can help you look inside the bones."

Such a thing exists???

"Hehe. I secretly borrowed my grandfather's precious magic magnifying glass."

"So this is supposed to reveal *everything*...?"

"Of course."

44   A Journey into the Human Body

This looks like fun.

Wow... It's true.

Hey! Get that thing away from me!

It's no different from your own body. There's nothing to see here...

What's inside my body is top secret! No one must look inside!!

Shall we see what Ken really looks like?

Bone 45

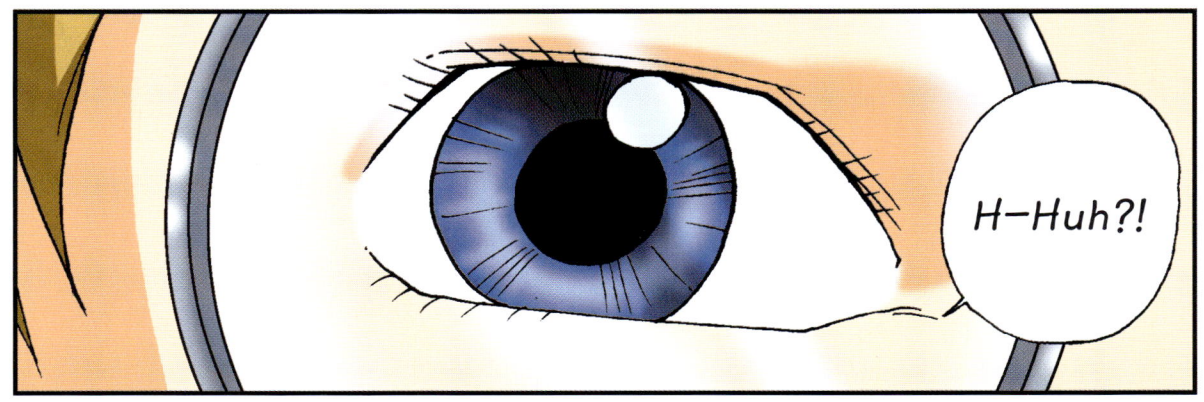

Quack!

What's the matter with him?

What could be inside his body for him to act like such a lunatic?

Joon, when are you going to look inside the bones? I'm curious to know what's inside.

Okay. Let's take a look.

H-Huh?!

46   A Journey into the Human Body

There are holes inside the bone??

What? It's full of holes?

Is it because the skeleton is made of chicken bones??

No, these are human bones. The holes make the bone stronger and lighter.

Yes. On the surface, it looks smooth, but it's actually full of small holes, kind of like a fisherman's net.

Yuna's right. The holes inside the bones make them lighter.

If your bones were solid, you'd have a hard time swimming.

Bone 47

"I see... And bird bones are even lighter because they are also hollow."

"Oh, otherwise it would be hard to fly."

"Right. Now look closer—the dense areas of our bone contain a lot of calcium."

"Inside the bones we have a watery substance called the bone marrow."

"Bone marrow sounds familiar."

"Of course, you've probably heard the word on TV..."

"...when people talk about bone marrow transplants..."

The bone marrow is where blood is made.
If something goes wrong here, we might be able to fix it with a bone marrow transplant.
That's right. That's what I've heard.
I didn't know the bones did so much.
Yes, bones have many functions.

50 A Journey into the Human Body

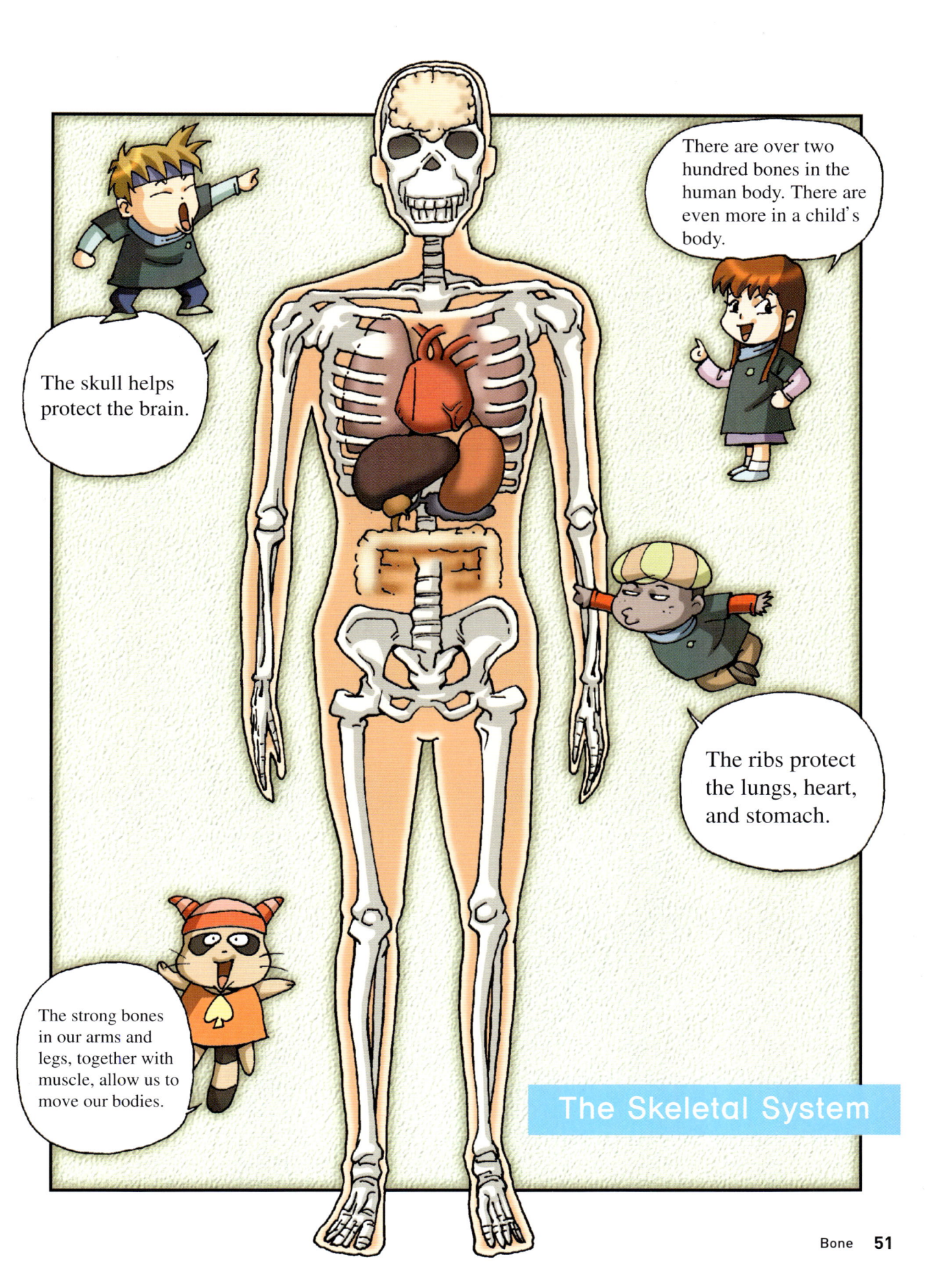

There are over two hundred bones in the human body. There are even more in a child's body.

The skull helps protect the brain.

The ribs protect the lungs, heart, and stomach.

The strong bones in our arms and legs, together with muscle, allow us to move our bodies.

The Skeletal System

The Stomach

So this is what the inside of a human body looks like.

BEEP BEEP

Look! The demon radar has finally detected the Shadow Demon.

52   A Journey into the Human Body

Where are we now?
The stomach?
The lungs?

Again, it's time for me to step up.

I am now going to introduce our stops along the way, so pay careful attention.

Wow! It looks like a movie projector!

The Stomach 53

Wait! I have a question.

I heard the stomach can digest anything except metal and rock...and we're inside a pumpkin. Will we be safe??

This is the path we'll be taking to look for the demon. First, we'll go to the stomach, then to the small intestines, and finally to the large intestines.

Don't worry. This ship is protected by an invisible magic shield.

Well, sure, it hasn't been used in about two hundred years, but it should be okay.

What?? Two hundred years?! This thing belongs in a museum!

Ahhhhhh!!!

Help!! We're falling—

Hold on! I'll try to control this thing.

SPLASH

The Stomach 55

.....

Ugh... You're the pilot, remember? You've got to keep your hands on the controls at all times.

Thank goodness we made it to the stomach in one piece.

We're inside the stomach now?!

It's a good thing the magic shield was working.

56   A Journey into the Human Body

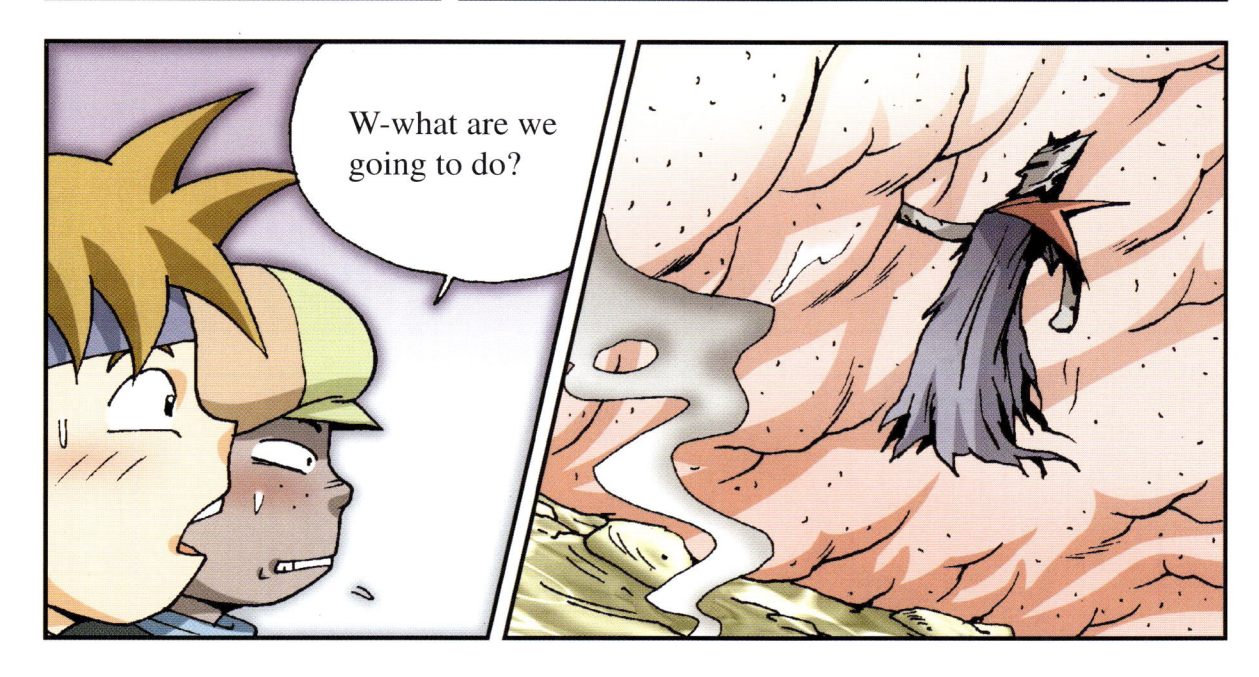

Look at that! Food is being digested.

Huh!!??

It's the Shadow D-d-demon!!? We're in trouble. We're not going to be able to fight right now...

W-what are we going to do?

The Stomach 57

A Journey into the Human Body

Shh! Quiet! He hasn't noticed us yet!

The ship is mixed in with the food. The demon is fooled because the ship looks like a pumpkin.

What is he doing?

What do you say we take him right now?

We can practice the spell we've been learning in class and turn him into a chicken.

This is no time for jokes.

Look!

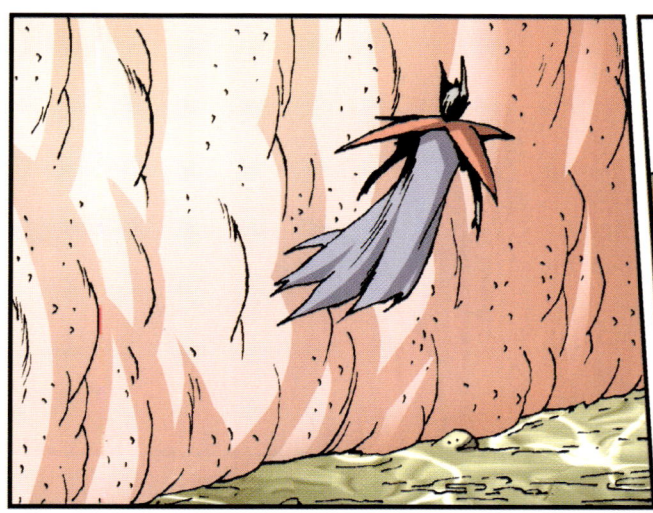

He's moving. We can't lose him.

Wait. Not yet. It's still too dangerous!

Let's quietly follow him for now and wait for the right moment.

Shh!

What's that?

I mean that liquid flowing down the stomach wall...

That's gastric juice.

Gastric juice is the digestive juice that is needed to digest food in the stomach.

Shh!

The gastric juice is dissolving the food!!

Of course! Gastric juice contains acid, and that's what helps dissolve the food!

Wouldn't that dissolve our own stomachs??

Ho ho— Yuna, you're really smart.

The stomach constantly makes a slimey mucus to protect itself from being digested!!

60   A Journey into the Human Body

It's too late. We've fallen into the digestive process. Oh no... What will happen to us?

Whoa!

Hold on tight, nothing will happen to us!

Ken! How long do we have to endure this?

Well, digestion can last five hours in the stomach!

What?! We've got to put up with this for five more hours?!!

The Stomach 61

How Food Travels through the Body

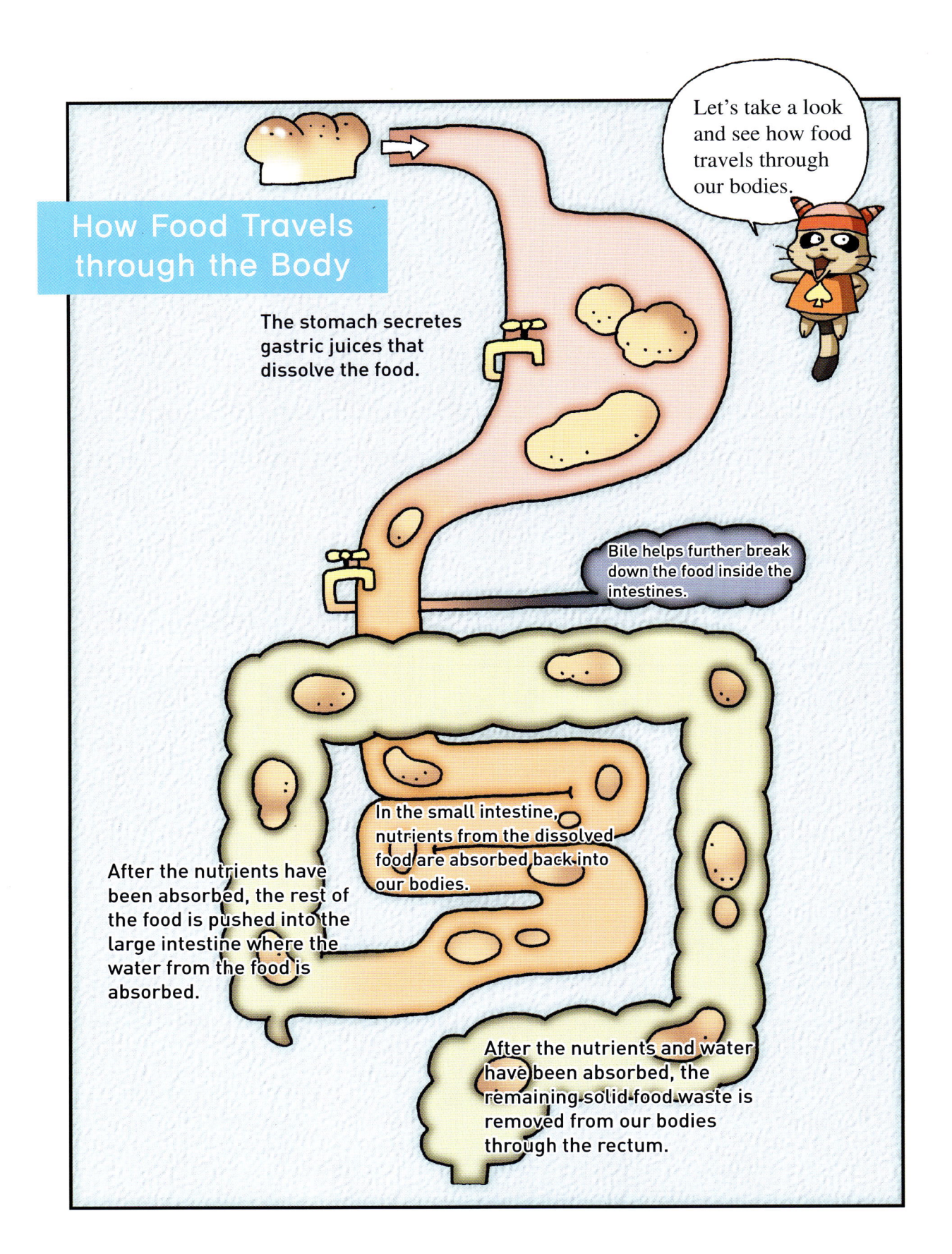

Let's take a look and see how food travels through our bodies.

The stomach secretes gastric juices that dissolve the food.

Bile helps further break down the food inside the intestines.

In the small intestine, nutrients from the dissolved food are absorbed back into our bodies.

After the nutrients have been absorbed, the rest of the food is pushed into the large intestine where the water from the food is absorbed.

After the nutrients and water have been absorbed, the remaining solid food waste is removed from our bodies through the rectum.

How the Stomach Works

Gastric juices are secreted by the lining of the stomach, and these juices break down the food in the stomach.

1. Gastric juices are sprayed over the food.

2. The stomach walls pop in and out, mixing and churning the food with gastric juices, turning the food into thick liquid.

The stomach's job is to mix and mash the food for digestion. The stomach looks like a large pocket. It does many things. For example, it produces gastric juices containing a strong acidic liquid that digests food and can kill germs that enter through the food. The stomach wall also secretes mucus to protect the stomach so it won't digest itself.

The Small Intestine

Hold on!

I think I'd better turn up...

...the magic power!

We made it!!

The Small Intestine 65

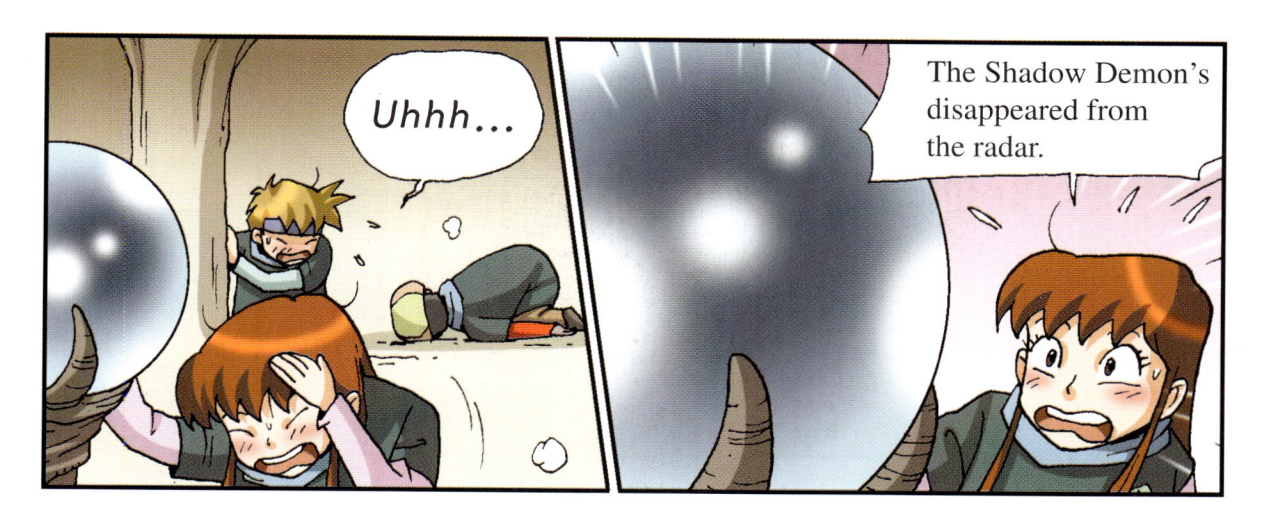

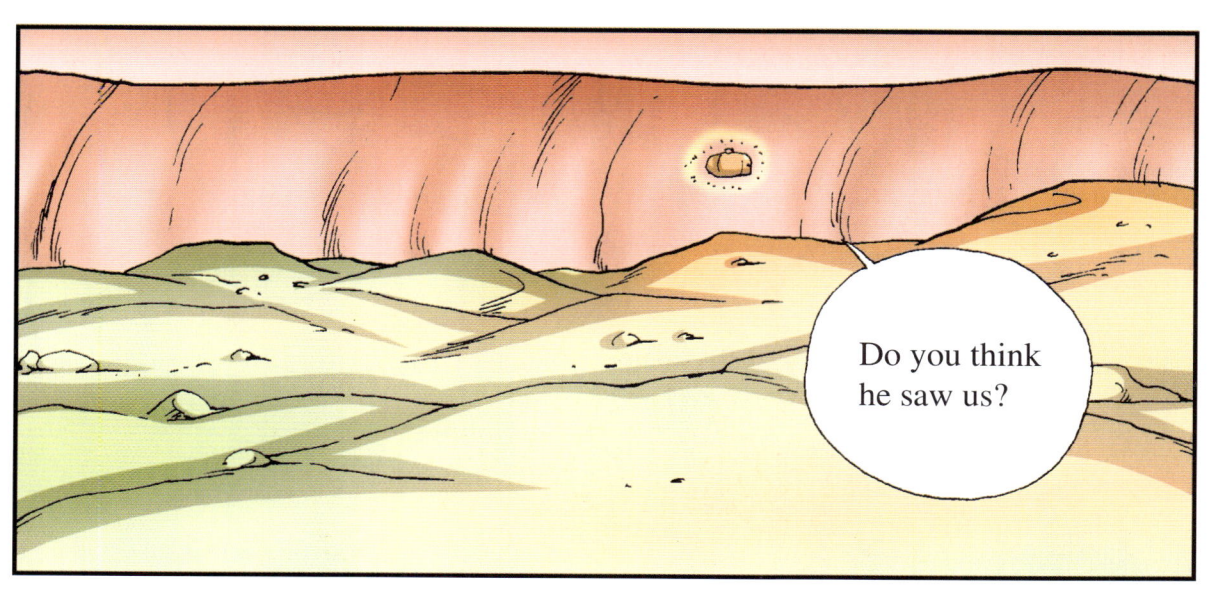

Oh...how boring. Ken, how much longer do we have to go?

At this speed I'd say about two more hours and we'll be out.

What!! Another two hours!!

Whew...the intestine is longer than I thought.

The small intestine, which we are passing through now, is quite long because it needs to absorb nutrients.

It's a whopping twenty feet long!

66   A Journey into the Human Body

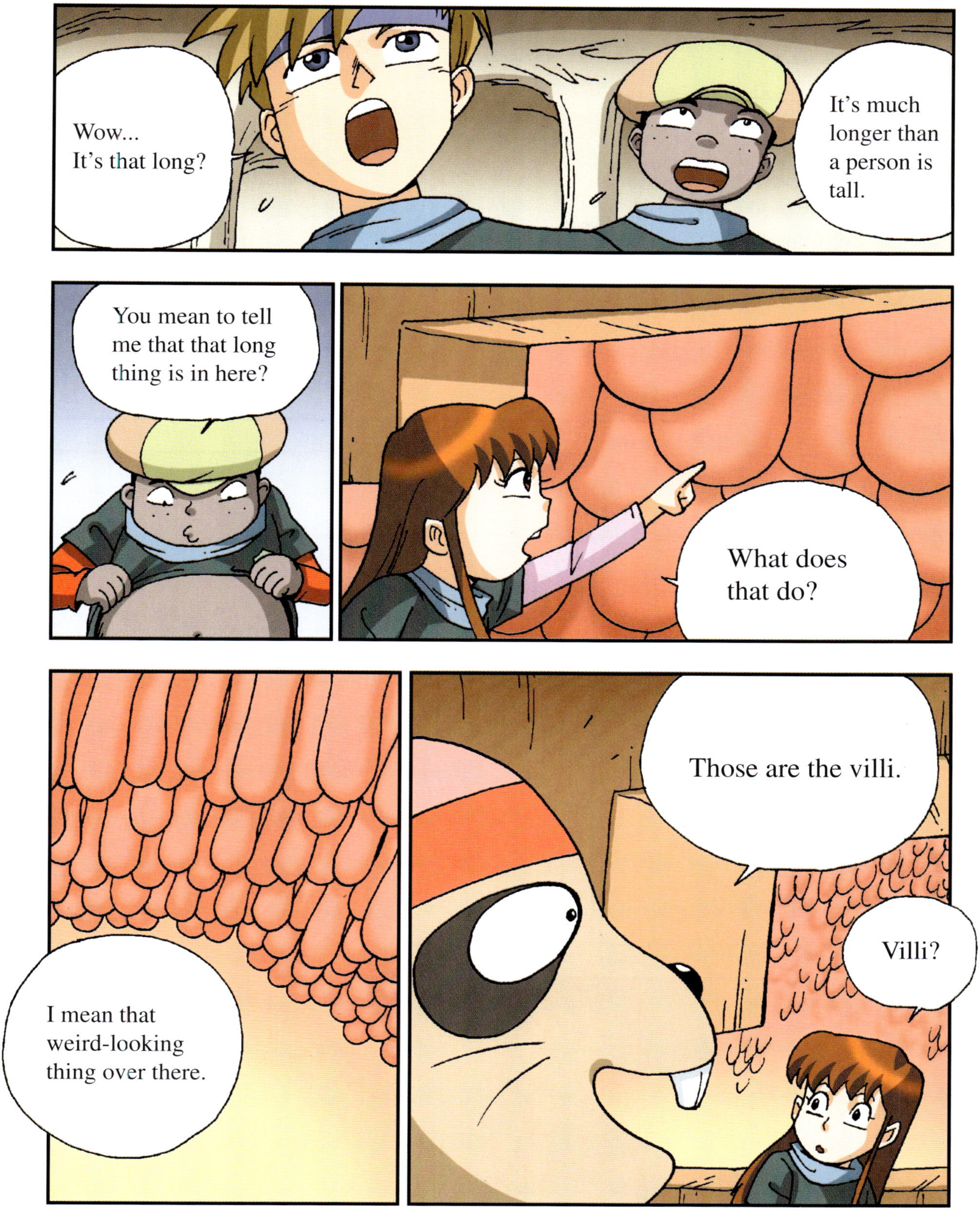
Wow...
It's that long?
It's much longer than a person is tall.
You mean to tell me that that long thing is in here?
What does that do?
I mean that weird-looking thing over there.
Those are the villi.
Villi?

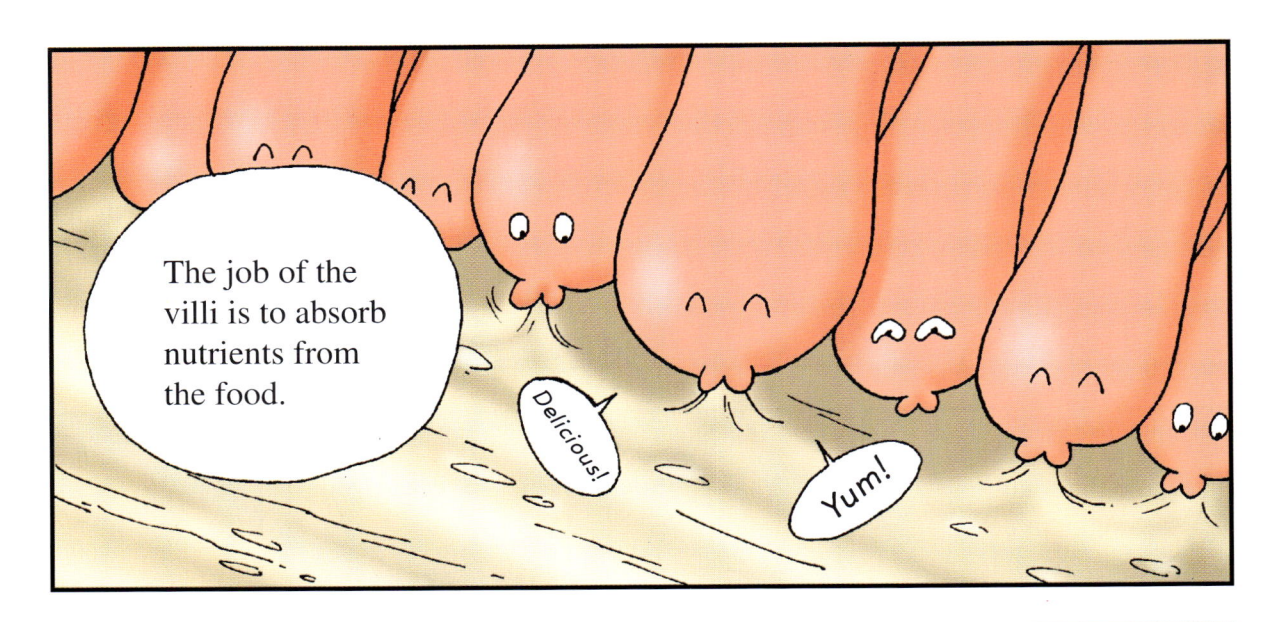

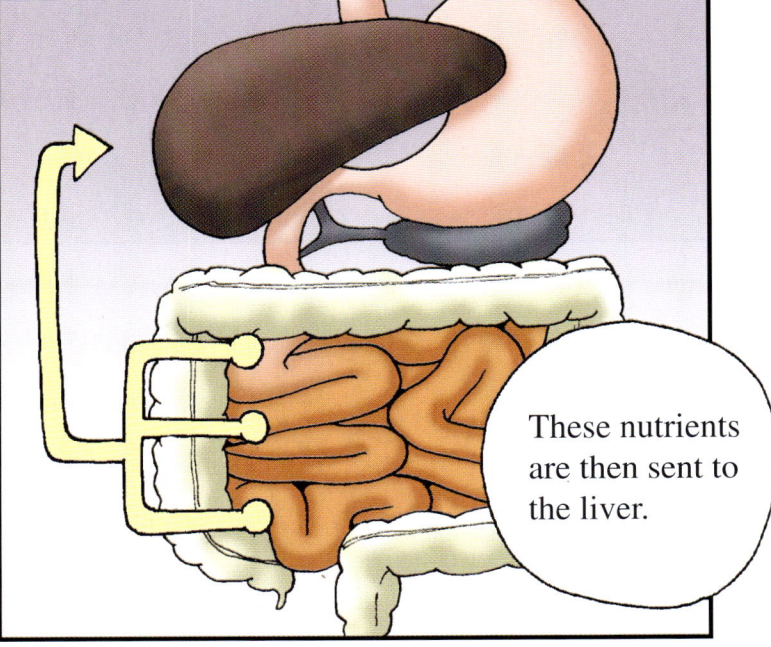

The job of the villi is to absorb nutrients from the food.

Delicious!

Yum!

There are many tiny blood vessels called capillaries inside the villi, and they absorb the nutrients from the digested food.

These nutrients are then sent to the liver.

So the villi play a very important role.

There's hardly a thing inside the human body that's not important.

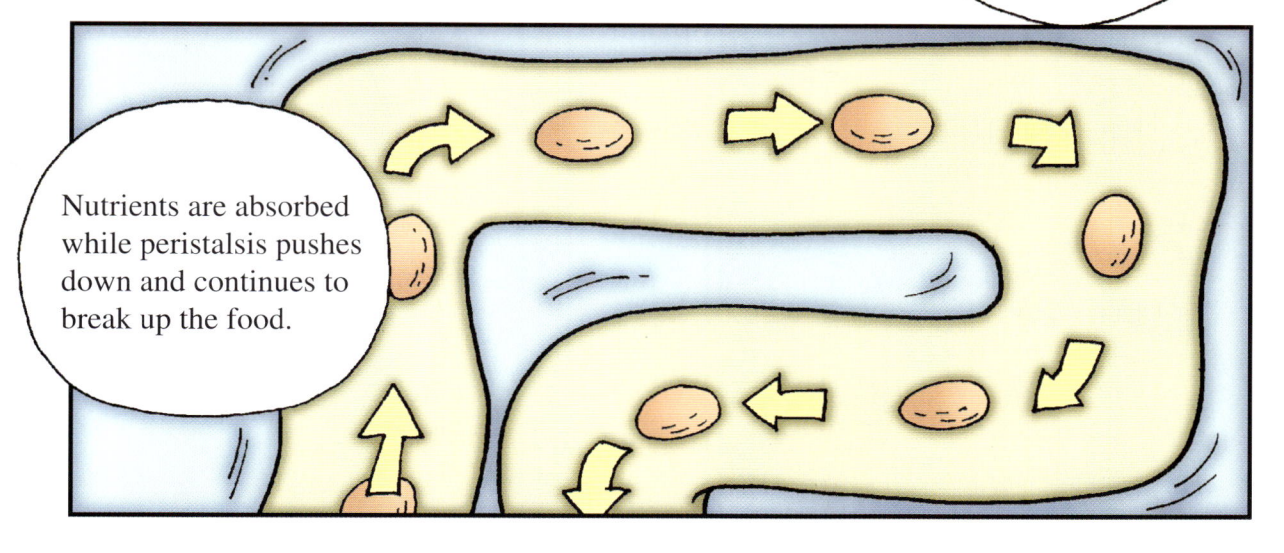

Ugh! What is it now!!

Haha. This is the movement of the intestine. It's called peristalsis.

And what is that??

Peristalsis is when the muscles squeeze, pushing the food through the small intestine.

Nutrients are absorbed while peristalsis pushes down and continues to break up the food.

The Small Intestine 69

It's a totally automatic system.
Yeah, and on top of that, it works perfectly without its owner noticing.
Sniff... What's that smell?
Yeesh...that stinks really bad. Joon, was that you?
What are you talking about? It definitely ain't me.
That is the smell of food being digested.
What...!!??
I can't even breathe because it stinks so much!!

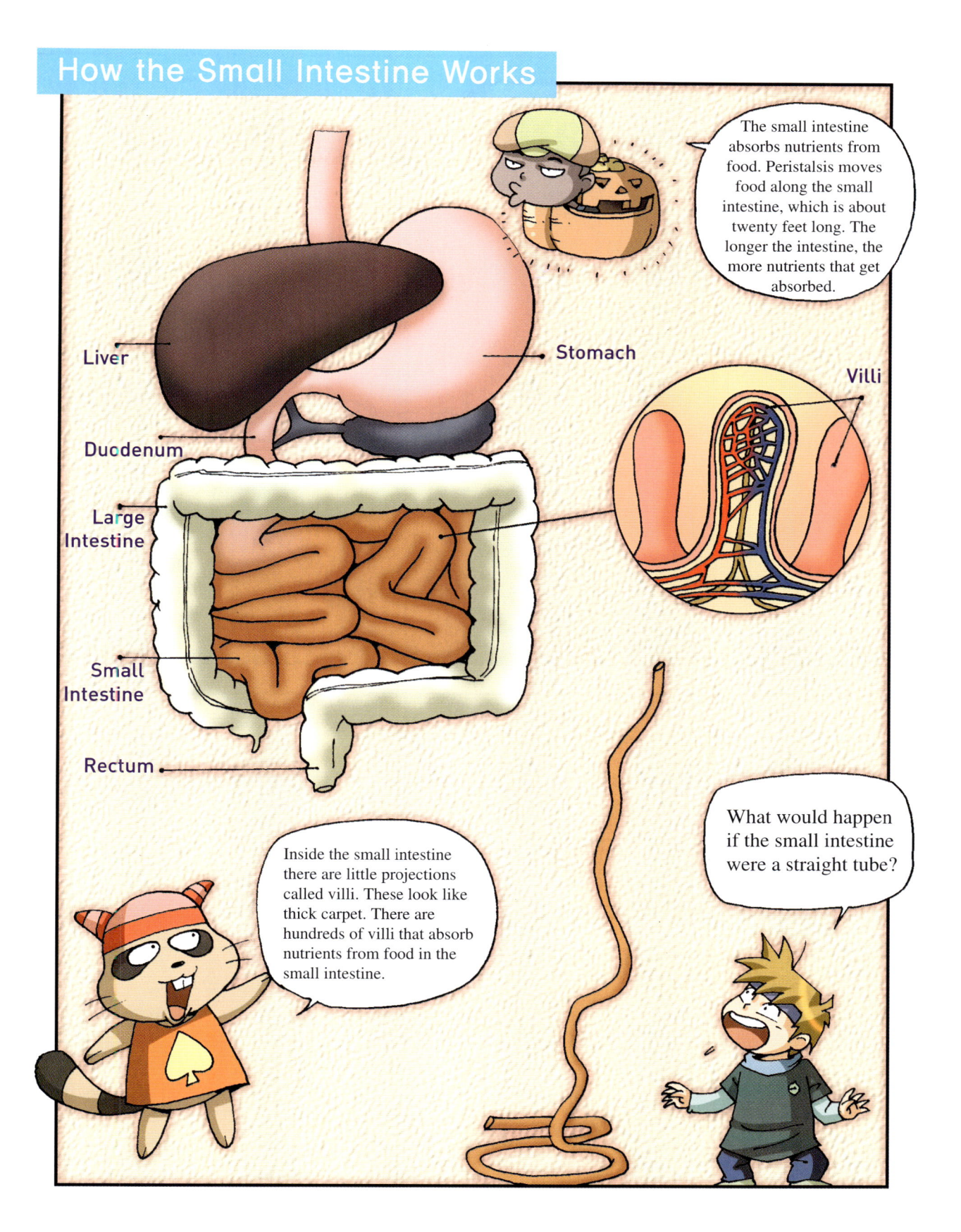

How the Small Intestine Works

The small intestine absorbs nutrients from food. Peristalsis moves food along the small intestine, which is about twenty feet long. The longer the intestine, the more nutrients that get absorbed.

Liver

Stomach

Villi

Duodenum

Large Intestine

Small Intestine

Rectum

Inside the small intestine there are little projections called villi. These look like thick carpet. There are hundreds of villi that absorb nutrients from food in the small intestine.

What would happen if the small intestine were a straight tube?

The Small Intestine 71

The Large Intestine

Ugh!

Whoa! The smell is lethal.

I can still smell it even though my nose is stuffed.

I don't think the demon would be anywhere in here.

As wicked as he may be, the demon would probably suffer just as much as we are.

Still, we have to look around carefully.

Does the large intestine also absorb nutrients?

Probably. It seems to absorb the nutrients that the small intestine couldn't get to.

Heavens no... The large intestine's job is to absorb water from the digested food.

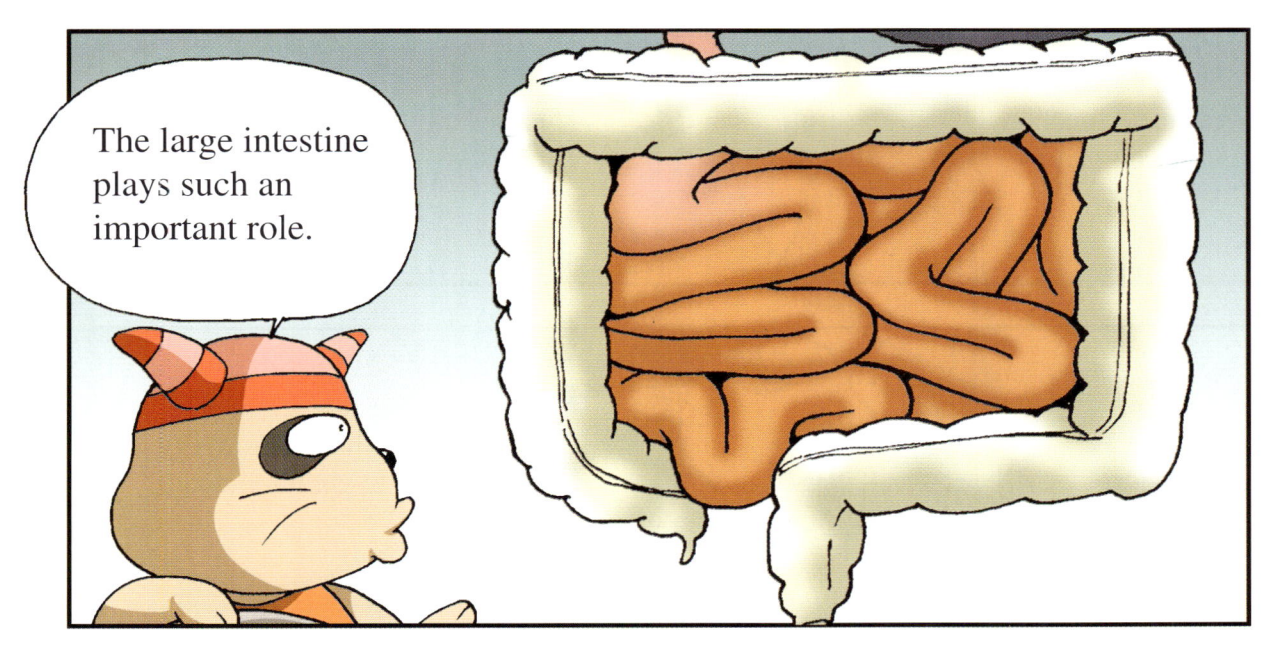

Absorb water??!!

You are aware that the human body is made up mostly of water, aren't you?

The large intestine plays such an important role.

The Large Intestine 73

74   A Journey into the Human Body

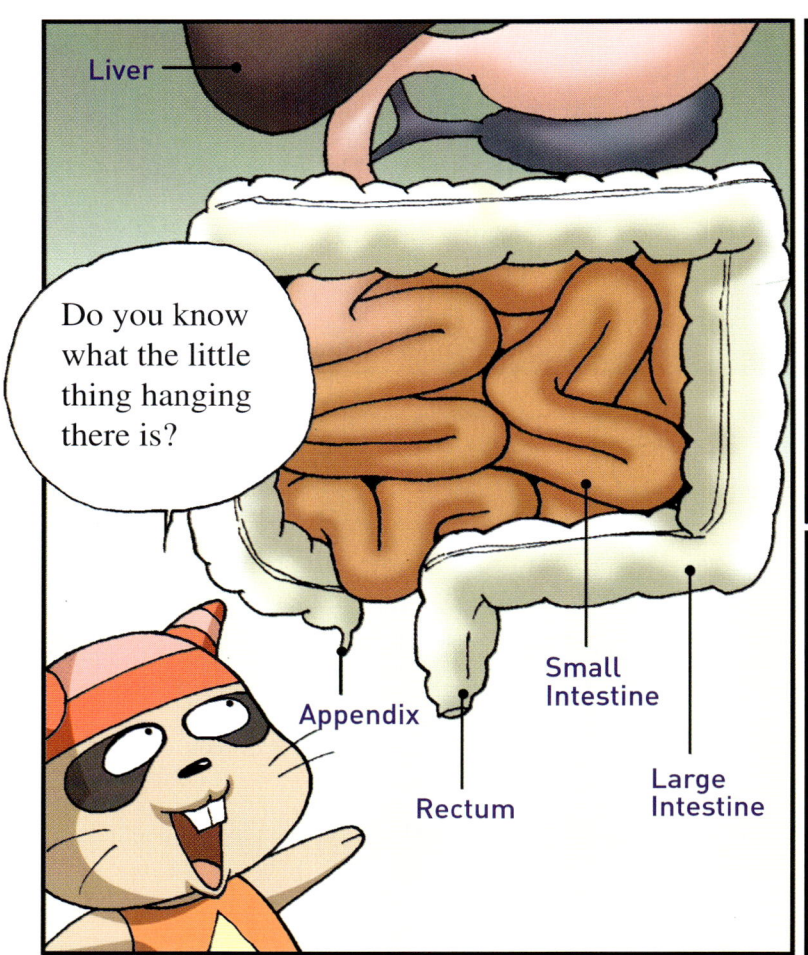

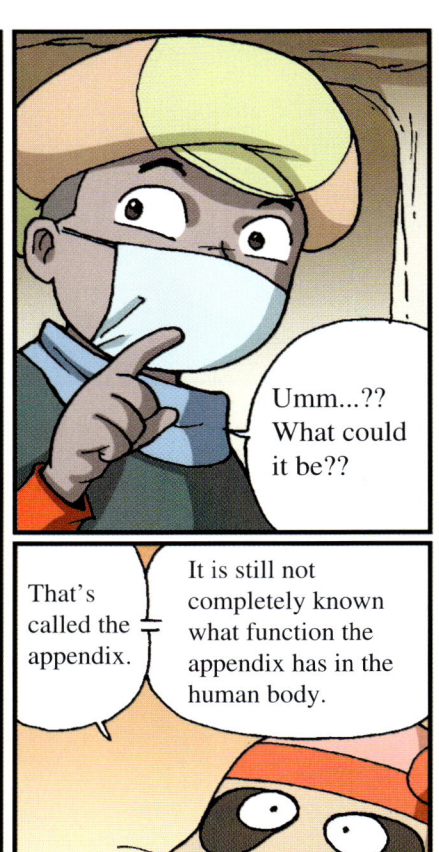

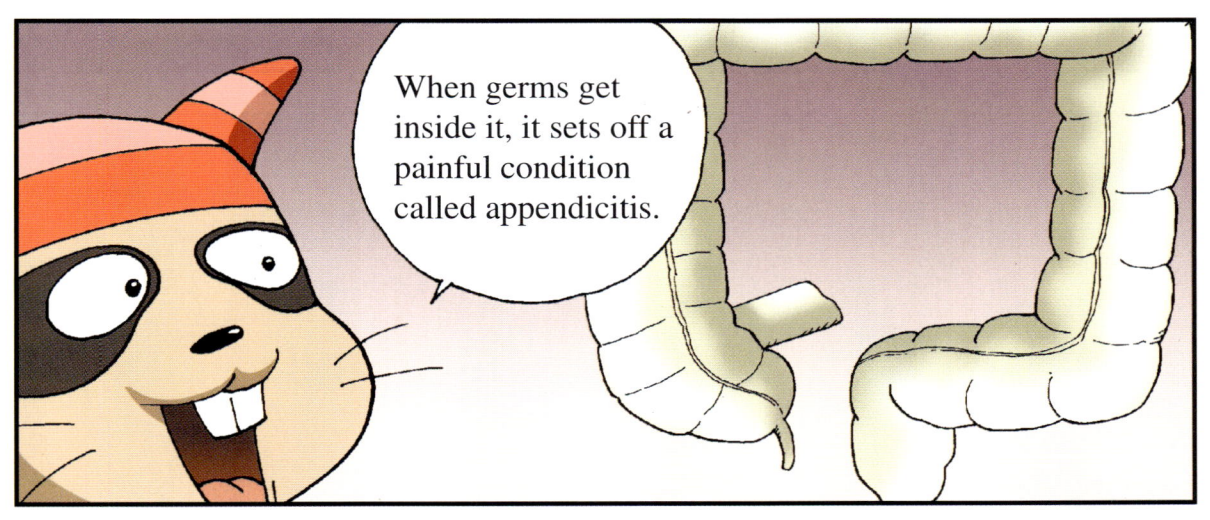

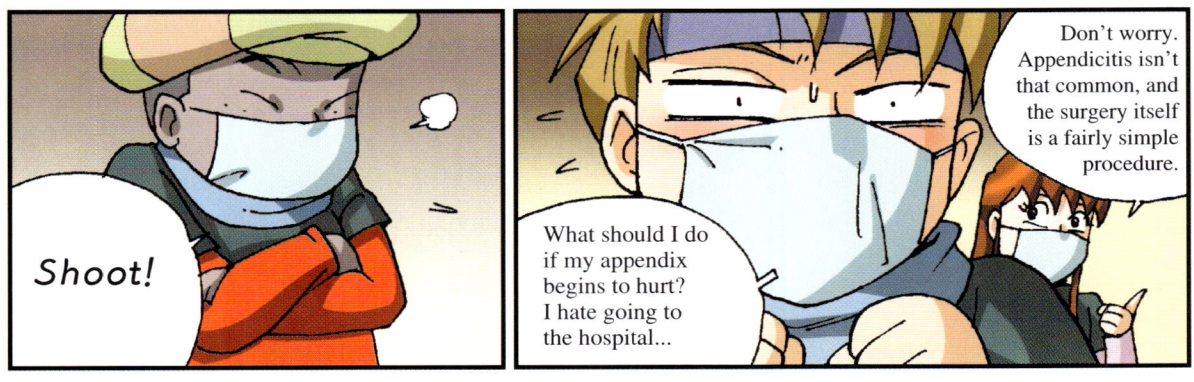

What...? How come??

When germs get inside it, it sets off a painful condition called appendicitis.

If that happens, the pain is severe... ...and requires surgery.

Shoot!

What should I do if my appendix begins to hurt? I hate going to the hospital...

Don't worry. Appendicitis isn't that common, and the surgery itself is a fairly simple procedure.

Ugh...that... m—monster!!

That's colon bacilli.

Yuck... That's nasty.

What... is...that?? It looks disgusting!!

There are many bacteria living in the large intestine. The colon bacillus is just one of them.

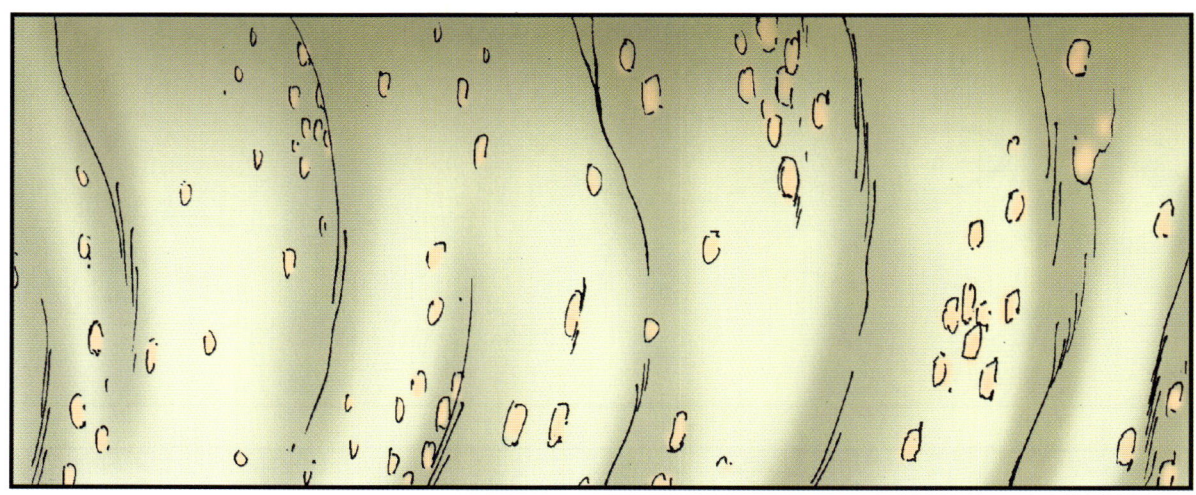

Aren't colon bacilli bad bacteria?

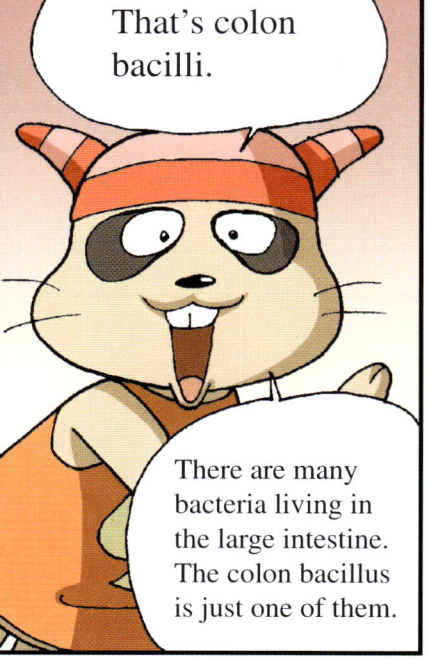

76   A Journey into the Human Body

I hear on the news sometimes about how dangerous they are, and some food sellers have gotten in trouble for selling food containing the bacteria.
You kids don't know the other side of it.
Bacteria like the colon bacilli in our large intestine also help us function properly.
What?? Explain that one to us...
Bacteria help us digest the fiber in the food.
I need you to digest the fiber.
You can count on us.

Then how come it's illegal to sell food containing the bacteria?

You can have the right number of bacilli, or you can have too much. Too much makes us sick. That's why we musn't sell or eat food containing too much bacteria.

Oh... I see.

WHOOSH

Yipes!!! What is it now!?!

Oww, my ears... What's going on?

Has the Shadow Demon appeared!?!

78 A Journey into the Human Body

Puhahaha.
It's the sound of a fart!!

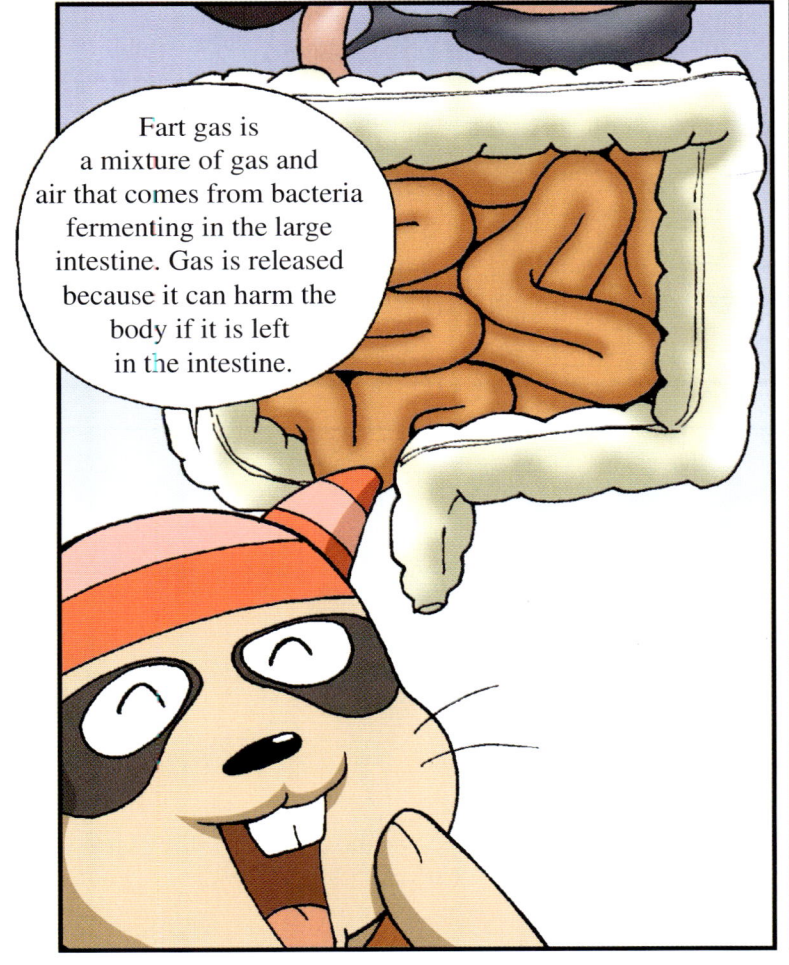

F-fart!!

Fart gas is a mixture of gas and air that comes from bacteria fermenting in the large intestine. Gas is released because it can harm the body if it is left in the intestine.

Whew...and I thought it was something else. The loud noise startled me.

Uh...well, then.

The Large Intestine

PRRRT

It's dangerous to leave it inside...

Woohoo... I feel much better now that I got rid of that harmful stuff.

Ugh... It's tough enough as it is in here without you adding to the smell!

What are you talking about? Would you rather have me get sick holding it in?

Ugh... Okay, fine.

80   A Journey into the Human Body

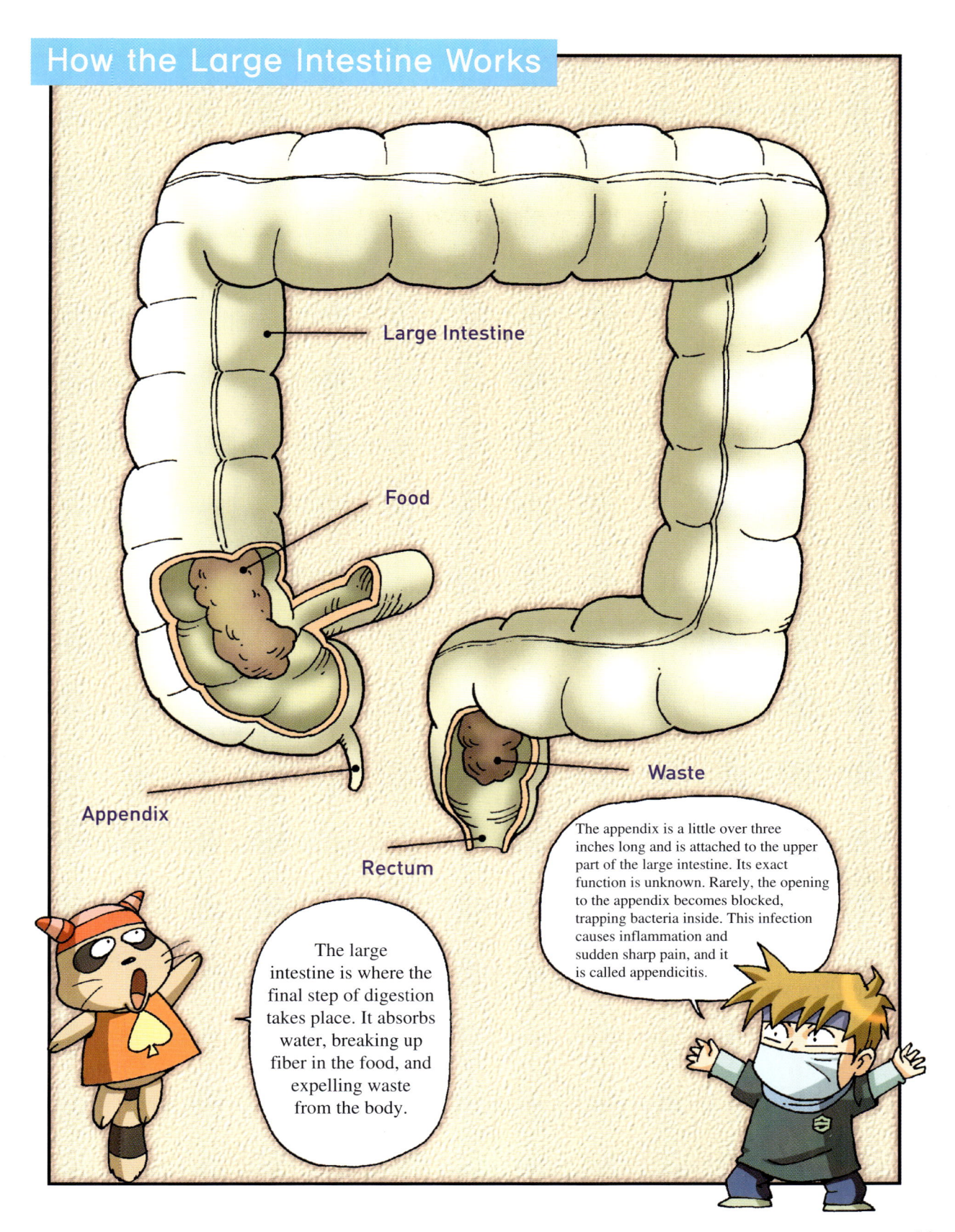

How the Large Intestine Works

Large Intestine

Food

Appendix

Rectum

Waste

The large intestine is where the final step of digestion takes place. It absorbs water, breaking up fiber in the food, and expelling waste from the body.

The appendix is a little over three inches long and is attached to the upper part of the large intestine. Its exact function is unknown. Rarely, the opening to the appendix becomes blocked, trapping bacteria inside. This infection causes inflammation and sudden sharp pain, and it is called appendicitis.

The Large Intestine **81**

The Lungs

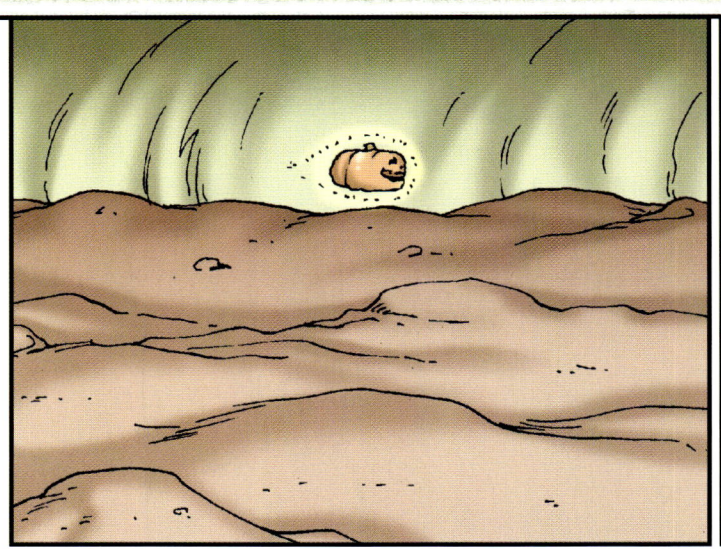

"I can't stand the smell."

"Soon we'll get to the end of the large intestine...and then what??"

"Yes!"

"D-don't tell me then we have to go back?"

"I'd rather die right here."

82   A Journey into the Human Body

Since the demon's not here, we'll have to go back.	Ohhhh...this smell is making my head hurt. No! No! No!
This is where magic comes in handy.	Let's go to where the demon is.

콜쓰리
눈피질
!!

The Lungs 83

84 A Journey into the Human Body

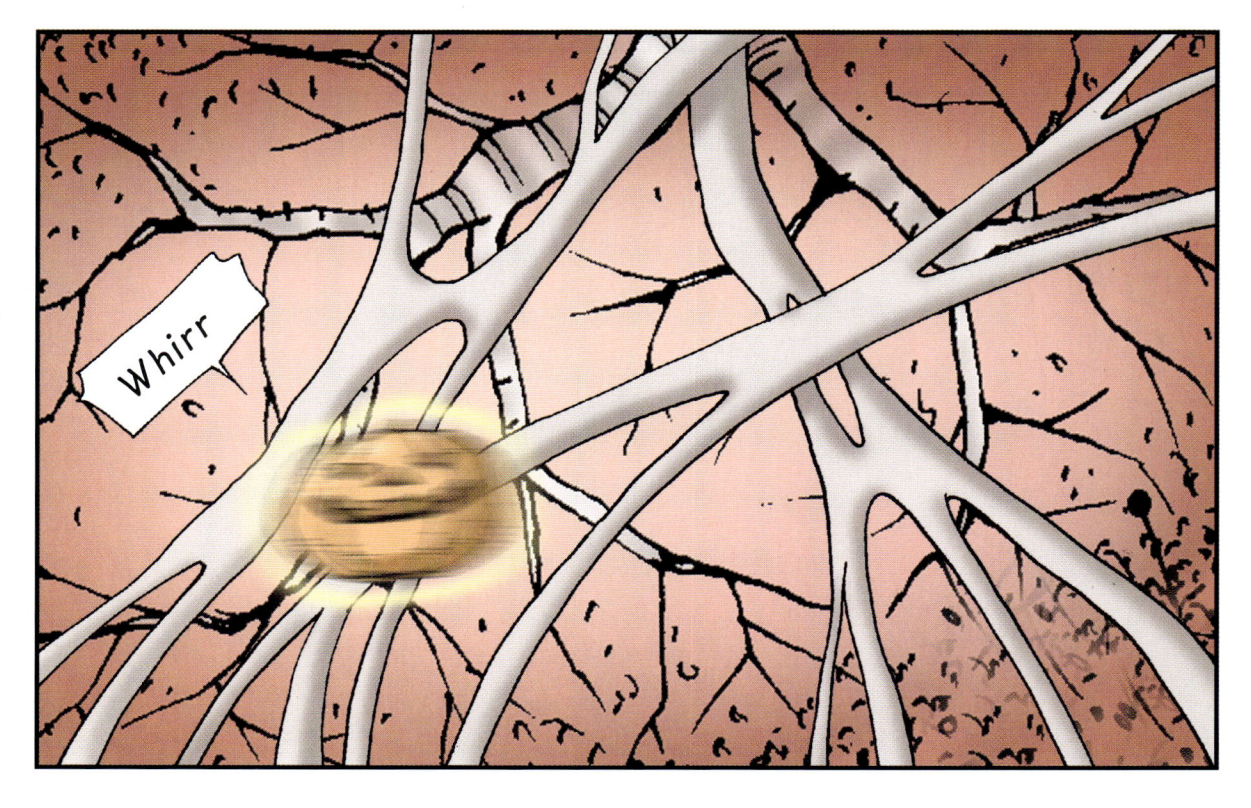

"We've made it to the lungs."

"The lungs?!"

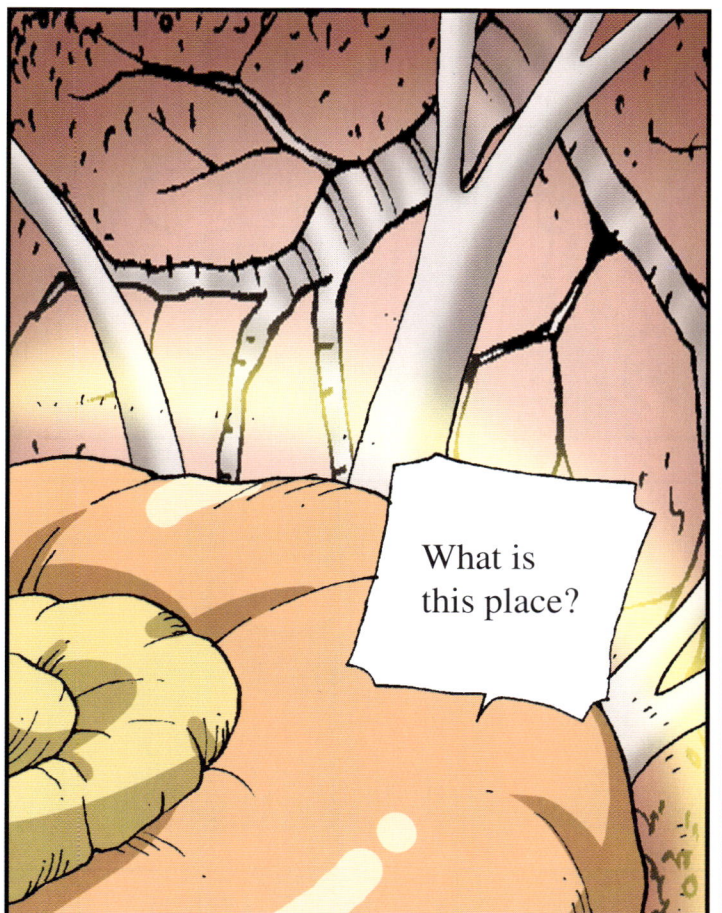

"What is this place?"

"Wow! It's huge! So this is the organ that supplies oxygen to our bodies. Look at it moving..."

Whew— "That's much better."

"I feel like we've entered a forest."

Thanks, Ken. That was just in time.

So how much air does a person need to survive?

An adult needs to breathe in about eight liters per minute. Children need ten liters per minute.

That's like five two-liter bottles of soda every minute!

And that's just during normal breathing. During exercise, you need much more.

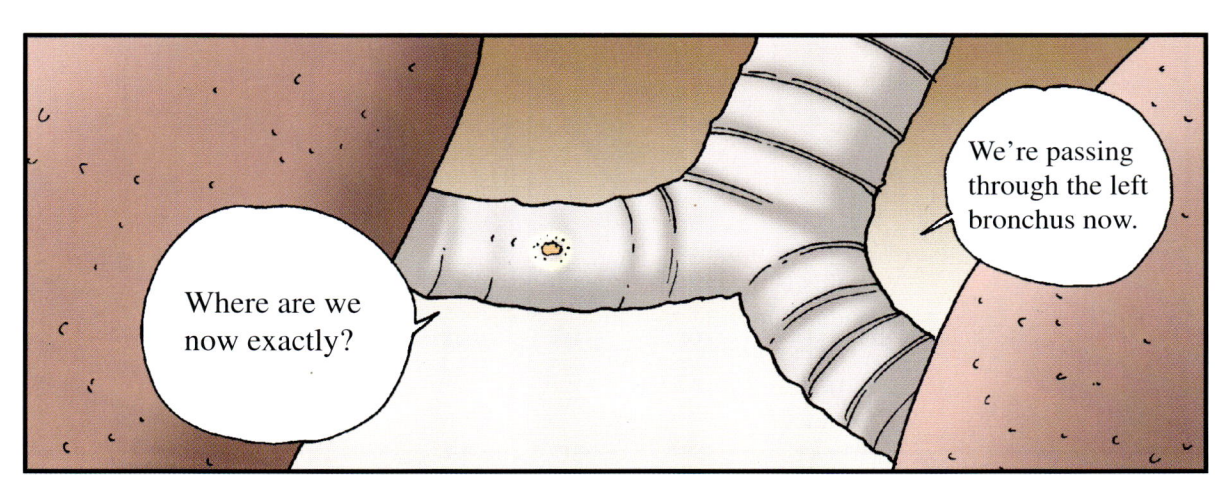

Where are we now exactly?

We're passing through the left bronchus now.

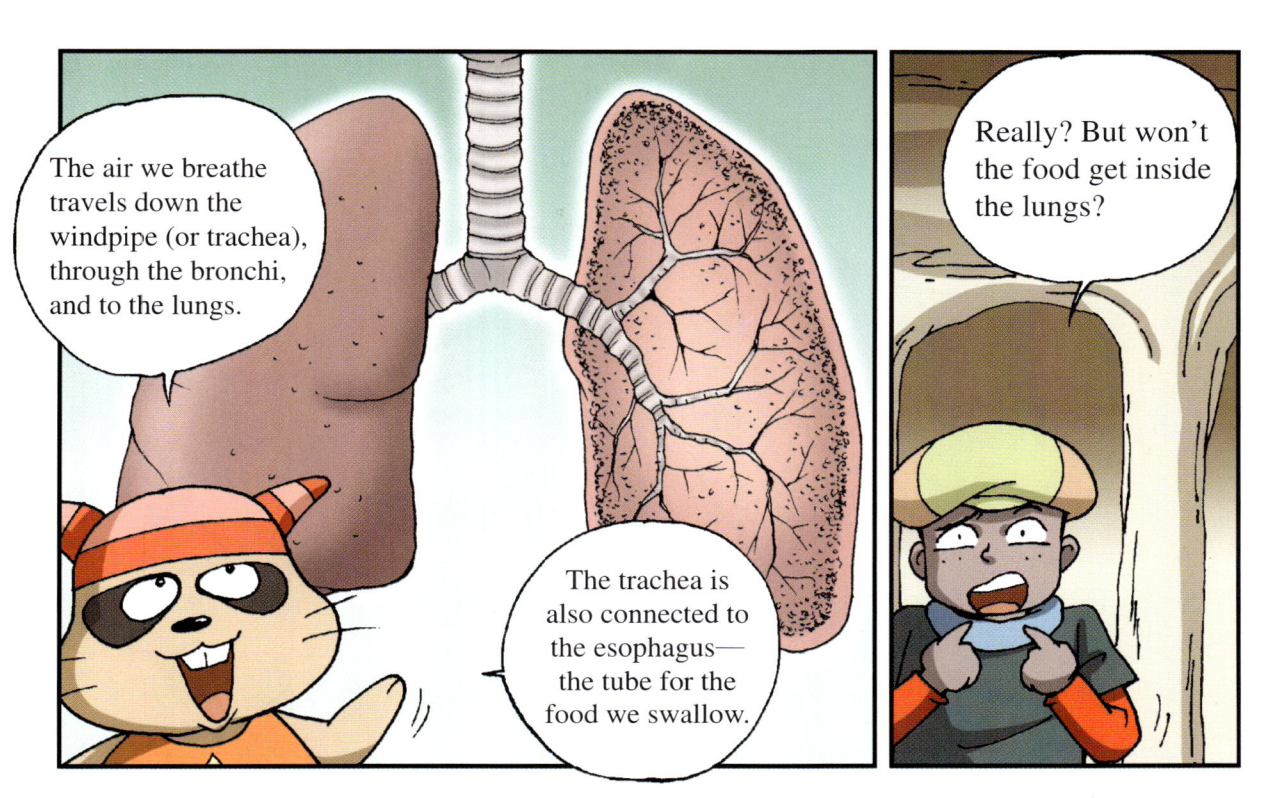

The air we breathe travels down the windpipe (or trachea), through the bronchi, and to the lungs.

The trachea is also connected to the esophagus—the tube for the food we swallow.

Really? But won't the food get inside the lungs?

No. This little flap here, called the epiglottis, stops the food from going down the wrong tube and into the lungs.

Wow— That's cool. They thought of everything!

Eww—What's that slimy stuff on the walls?

The Lungs 87

That's called a mucous membrane. It catches dirt and other things that don't belong in here, and it removes them from the body.
Is that the stuff they call phlegm?
Yes. After the mucous membrane collects the dirt, it is called phlegm.
Ewww—Can you imagine what'll happen if we breathe that stuff in...
Uh...where do we go from here?
These are the bronchioles.

All these paths look the same.
Which path should we take?
It doesn't matter because all paths lead to the same place.

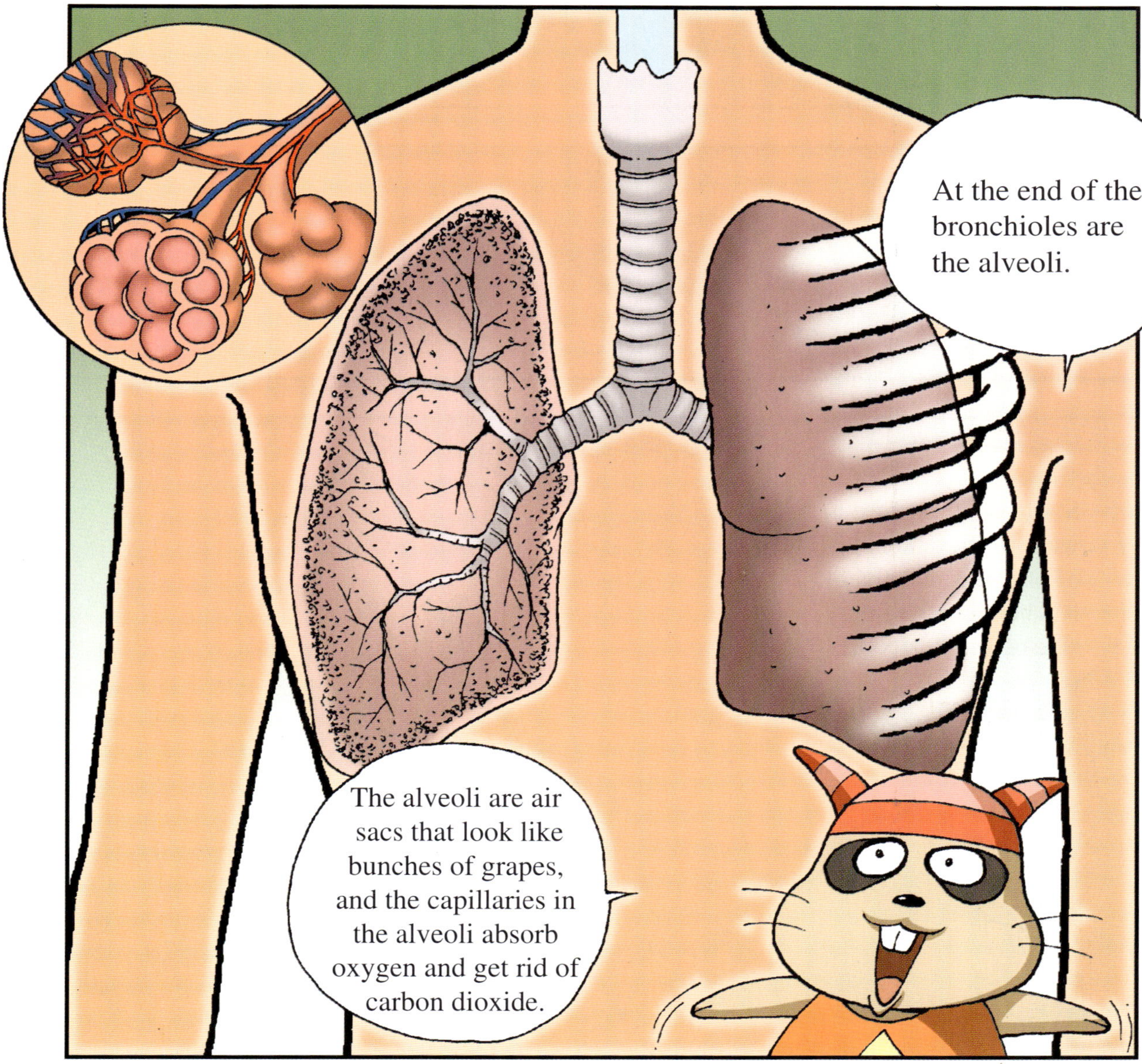
At the end of the bronchioles are the alveoli.
The alveoli are air sacs that look like bunches of grapes, and the capillaries in the alveoli absorb oxygen and get rid of carbon dioxide.

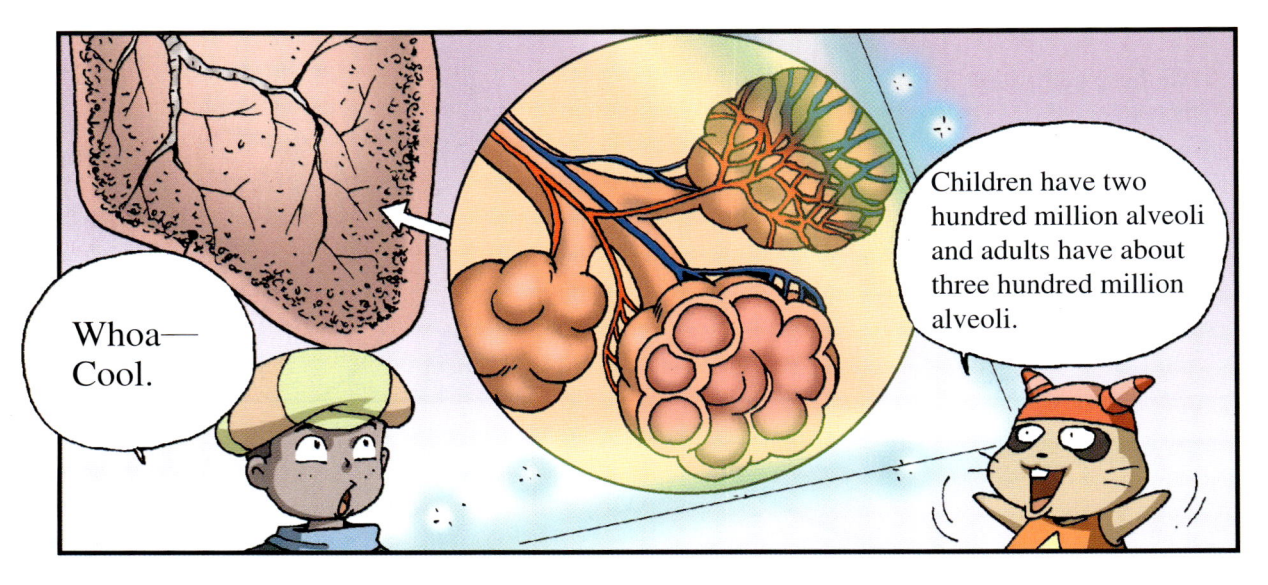

Whoa—Cool.

Children have two hundred million alveoli and adults have about three hundred million alveoli.

Two hundred million?

That's because the more alveoli there are, the more air we are able to breathe in.

Some say that if we were to stretch out all of one person's alveoli, it'd be about half the size of a tennis court.

Whoa — That's huge!

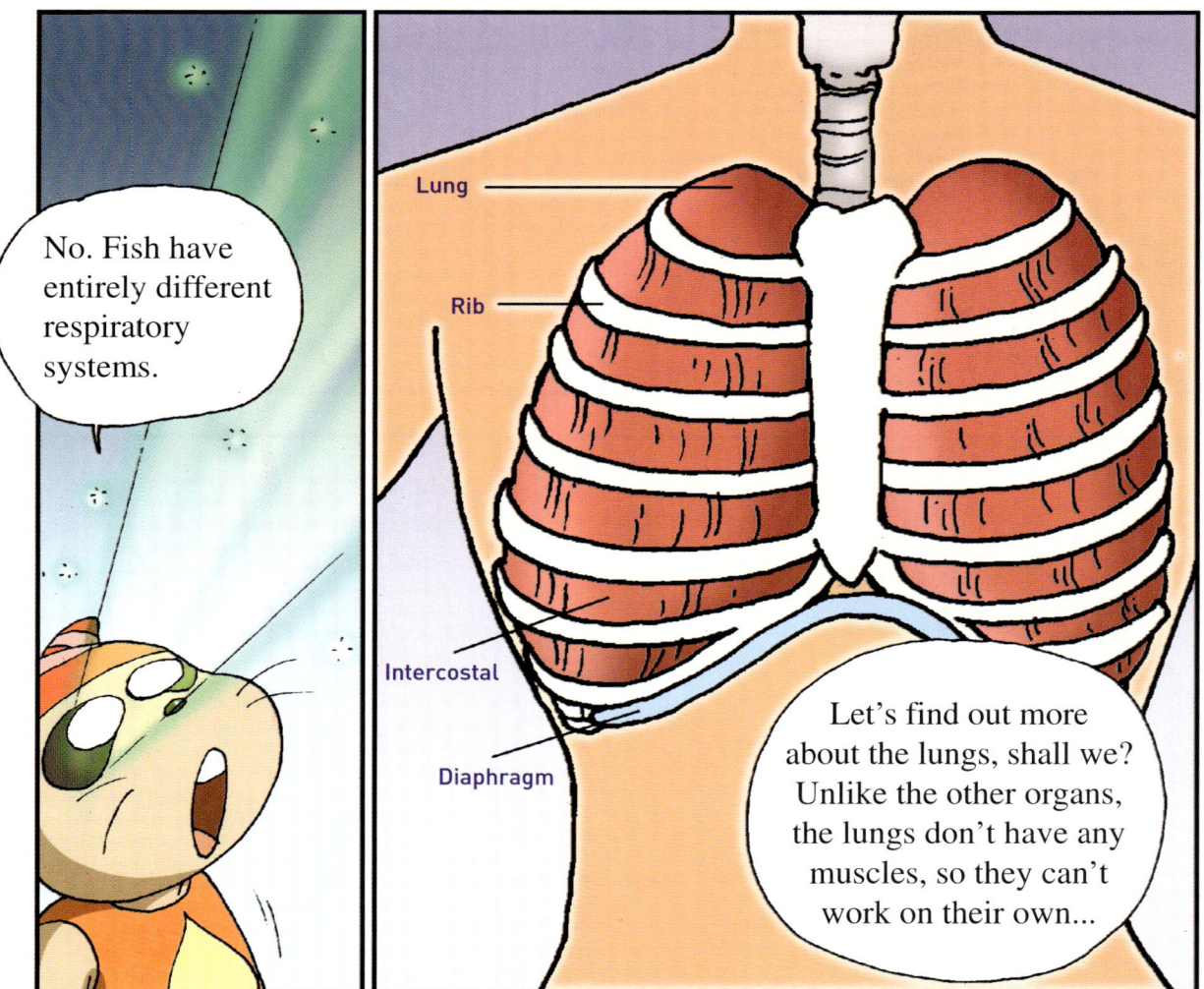

If the alveoli are unable to supply oxygen to the blood, even for a few minutes, we can die.

Wow— I guess the alveoli are really important..

Does that mean that fish have more alveoli than we do? Is that why they are able to live and breathe underwater?

No. Fish have entirely different respiratory systems.

Lung

Rib

Intercostal

Diaphragm

Let's find out more about the lungs, shall we? Unlike the other organs, the lungs don't have any muscles, so they can't work on their own...

The Lungs 91

Th-then, how do they move? Aren't lungs supposed to be moving all the time?

The muscles attached to the ribs help work the lungs.

Lung
Rib
Intercostal
Diaphragm

Those are the intercostal muscles over there...

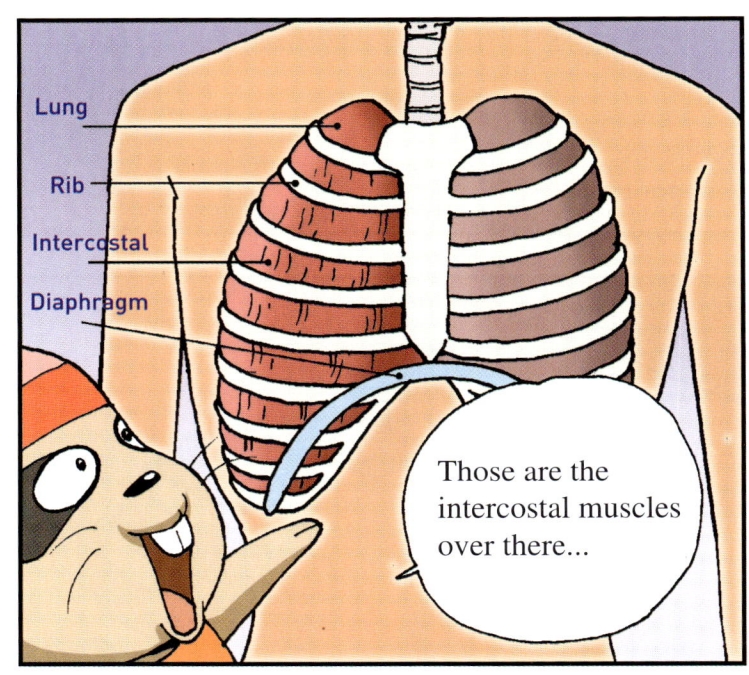

As these muscles expand and move out, the lungs expand, getting bigger and taking in air. This is what happens when we breathe in, or inhale. When the intercostal muscles contract, the lungs get smaller, and the air in the lungs is pushed out of the body. This is what happens when we breathe out, or exhale.

So is that what we're doing right now?

Not all breathing is done this way.

Really? What other kind of breathing is there?

92   A Journey into the Human Body

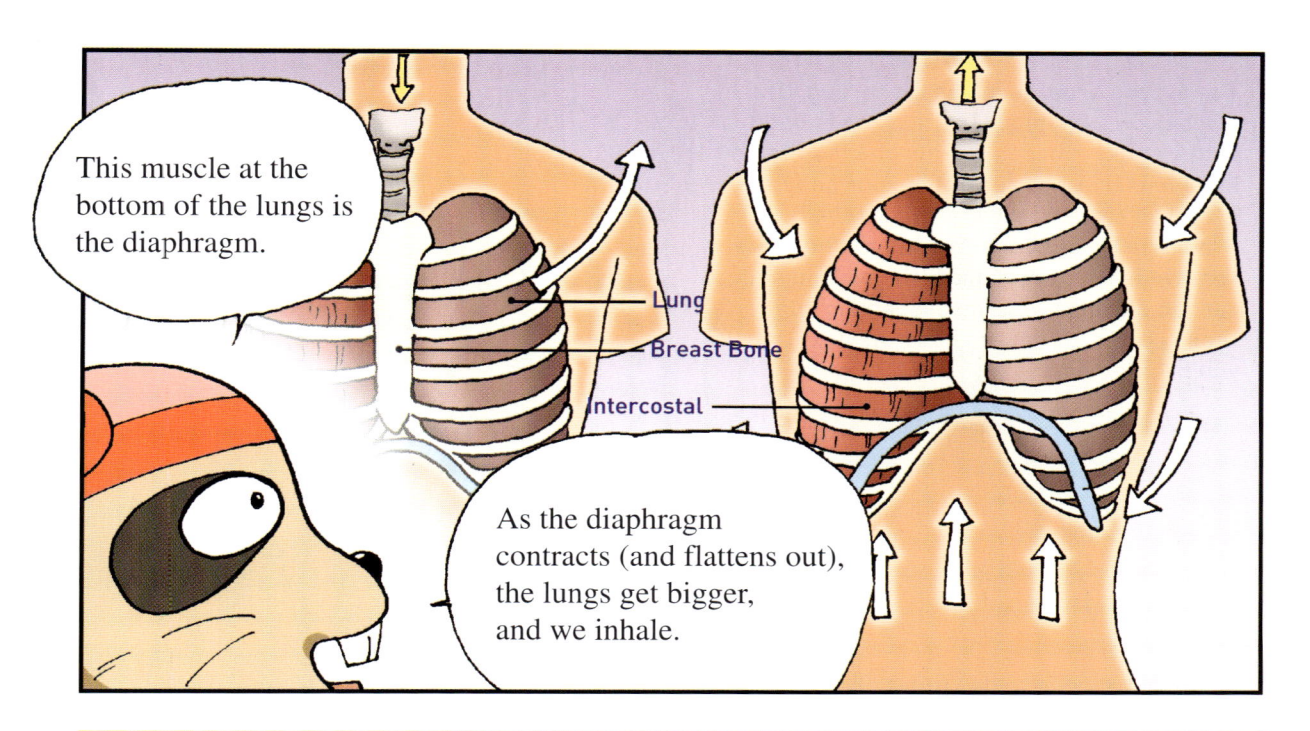

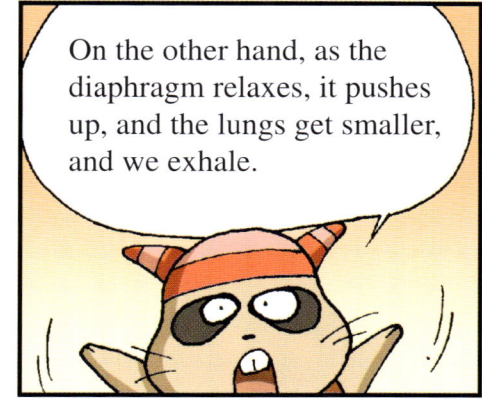

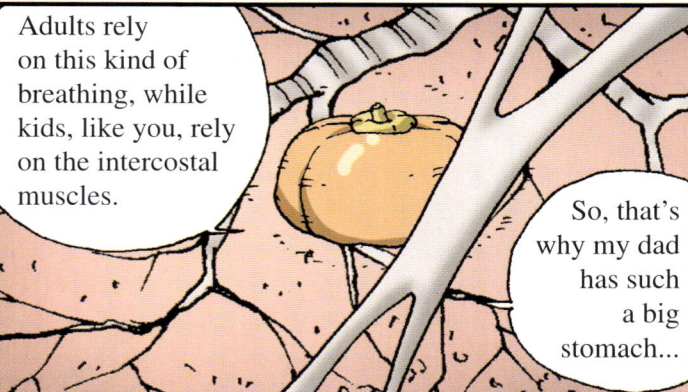

This muscle at the bottom of the lungs is the diaphragm.

Lung
Breast Bone
Intercostal

As the diaphragm contracts (and flattens out), the lungs get bigger, and we inhale.

On the other hand, as the diaphragm relaxes, it pushes up, and the lungs get smaller, and we exhale.

Adults rely on this kind of breathing, while kids, like you, rely on the intercostal muscles.

So, that's why my dad has such a big stomach...

BEEP BEEP

The demon radar's picked up on the demon!

The Lungs 93

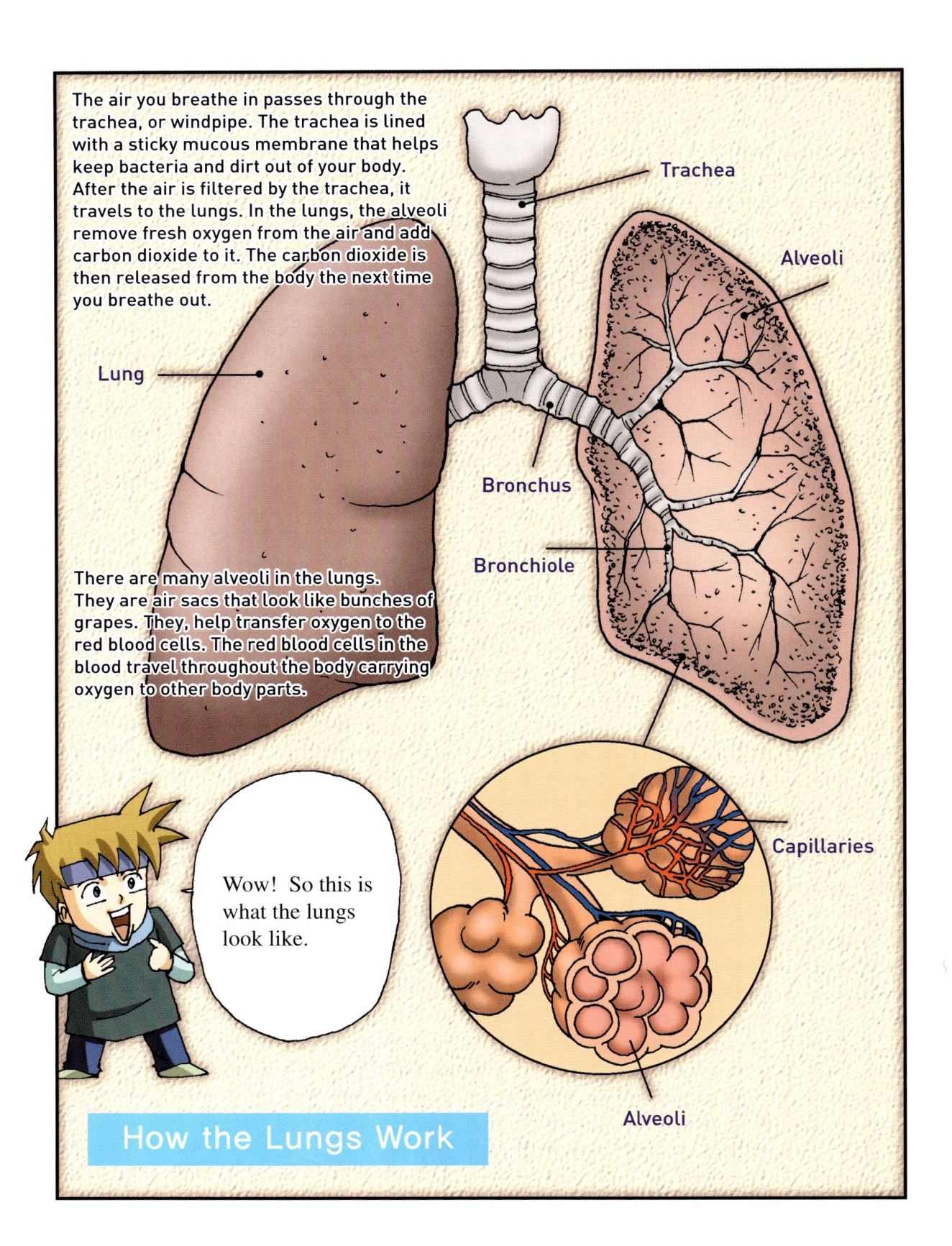

The air you breathe in passes through the trachea, or windpipe. The trachea is lined with a sticky mucous membrane that helps keep bacteria and dirt out of your body. After the air is filtered by the trachea, it travels to the lungs. In the lungs, the alveoli remove fresh oxygen from the air and add carbon dioxide to it. The carbon dioxide is then released from the body the next time you breathe out.

Trachea

Alveoli

Lung

Bronchus

Bronchiole

There are many alveoli in the lungs. They are air sacs that look like bunches of grapes. They, help transfer oxygen to the red blood cells. The red blood cells in the blood travel throughout the body carrying oxygen to other body parts.

Capillaries

Wow! So this is what the lungs look like.

Alveoli

How the Lungs Work

94   A Journey into the Human Body

Ribs move up.

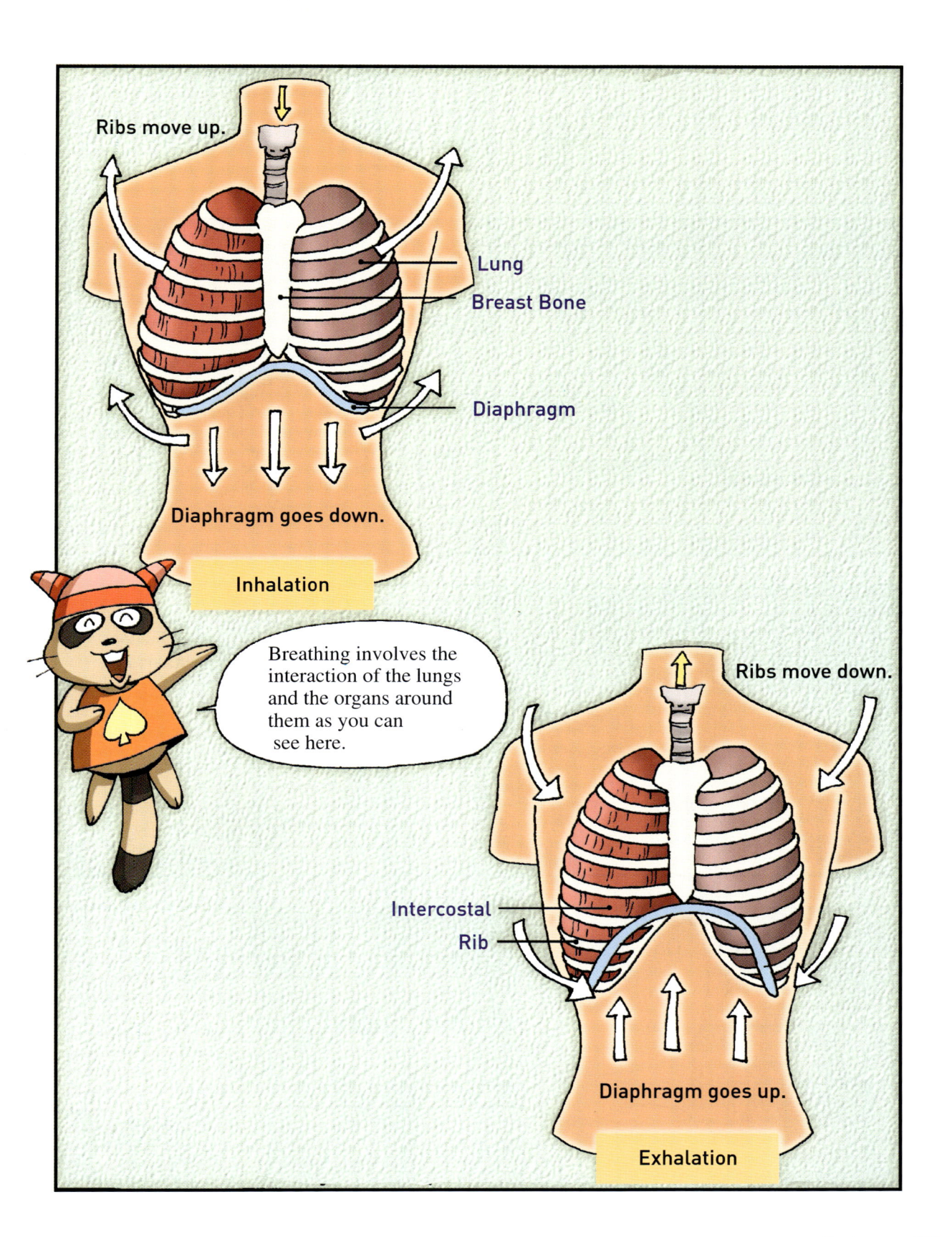

Lung
Breast Bone
Diaphragm

Diaphragm goes down.

Inhalation

Breathing involves the interaction of the lungs and the organs around them as you can see here.

Ribs move down.

Intercostal
Rib

Diaphragm goes up.

Exhalation

The Lungs 95

The Blood

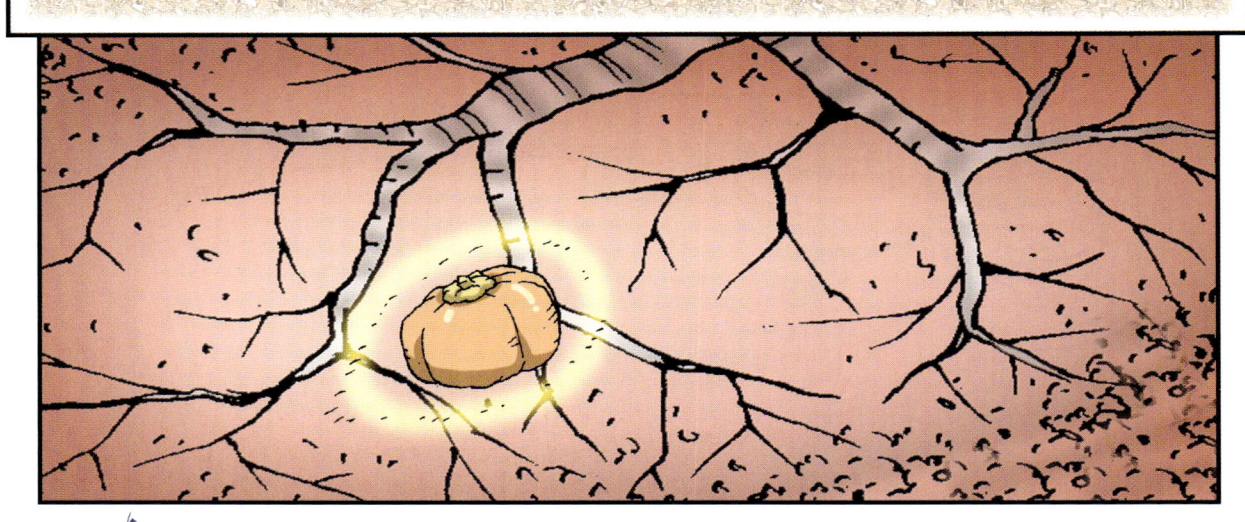

I think I see him!

The Shadow Demon is traveling along the blood vessels connected to the lungs.

Do you think he's realized that we're following him...?

That doesn't matter now. Let's follow him into the blood system!

A Journey into the Human Body

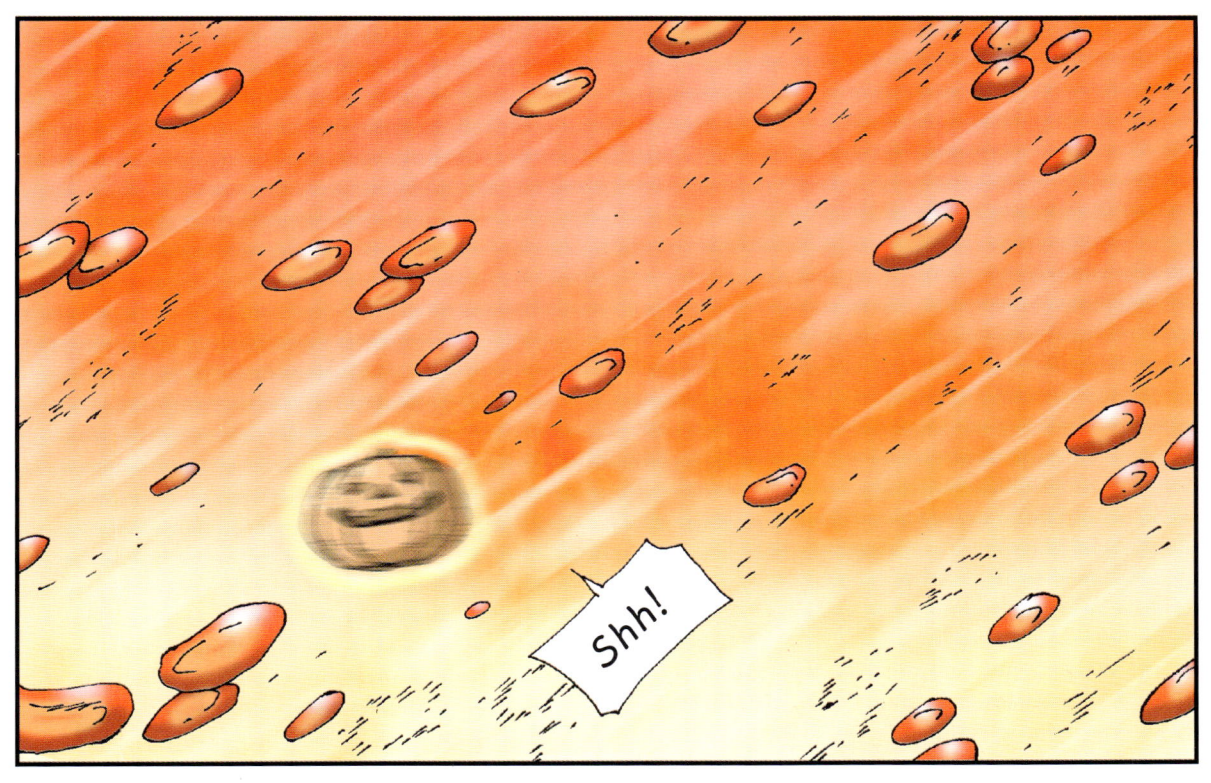

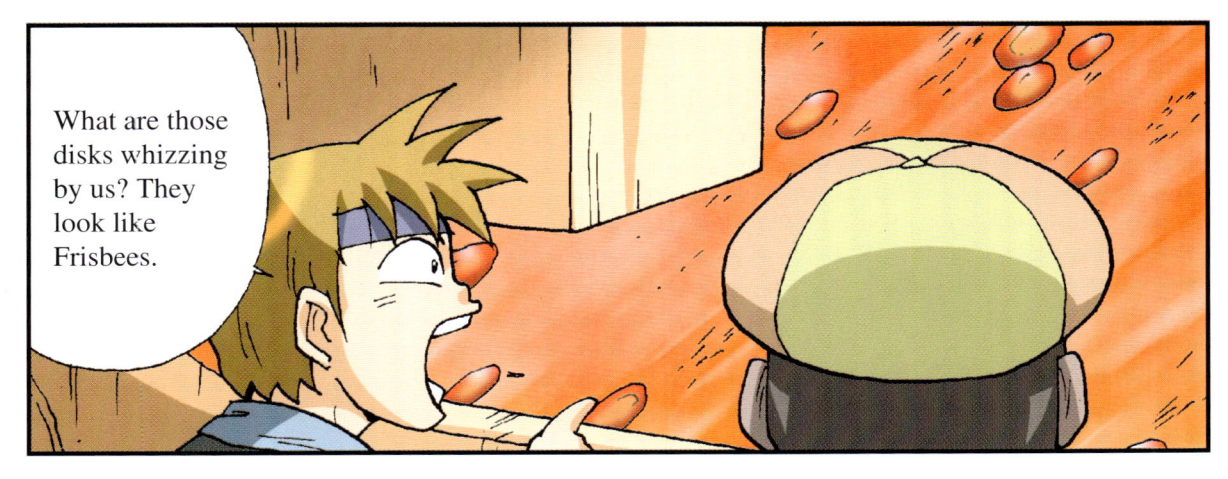

WHIRRRR

Shh!

What are those disks whizzing by us? They look like Frisbees.

The Blood 97

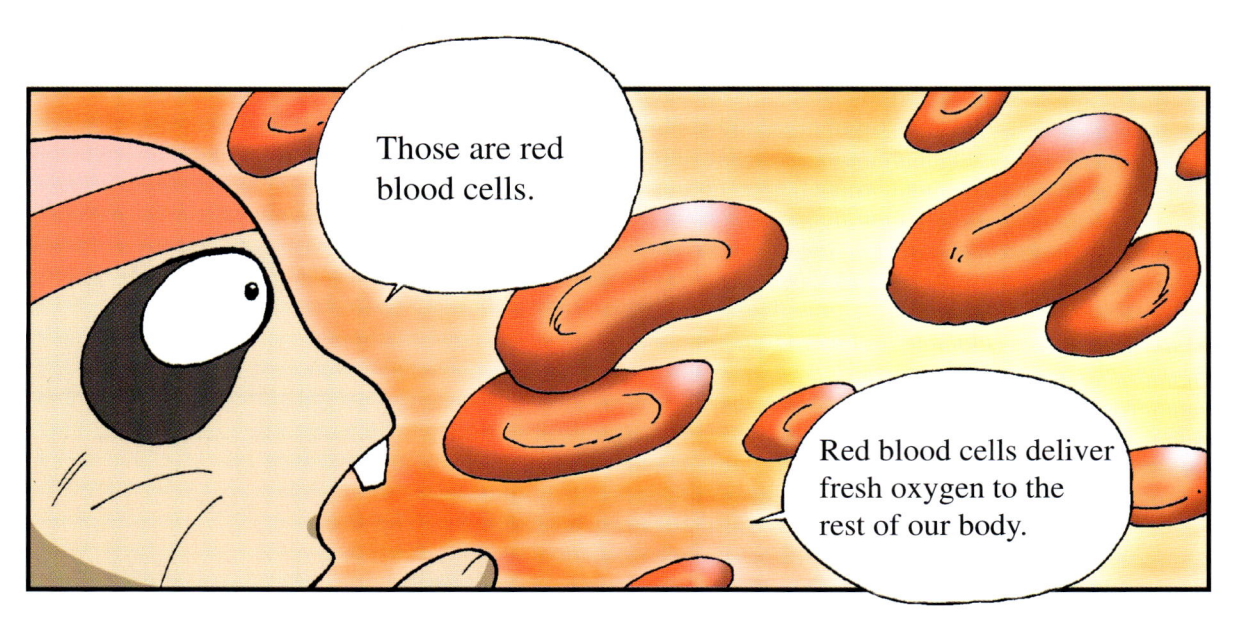

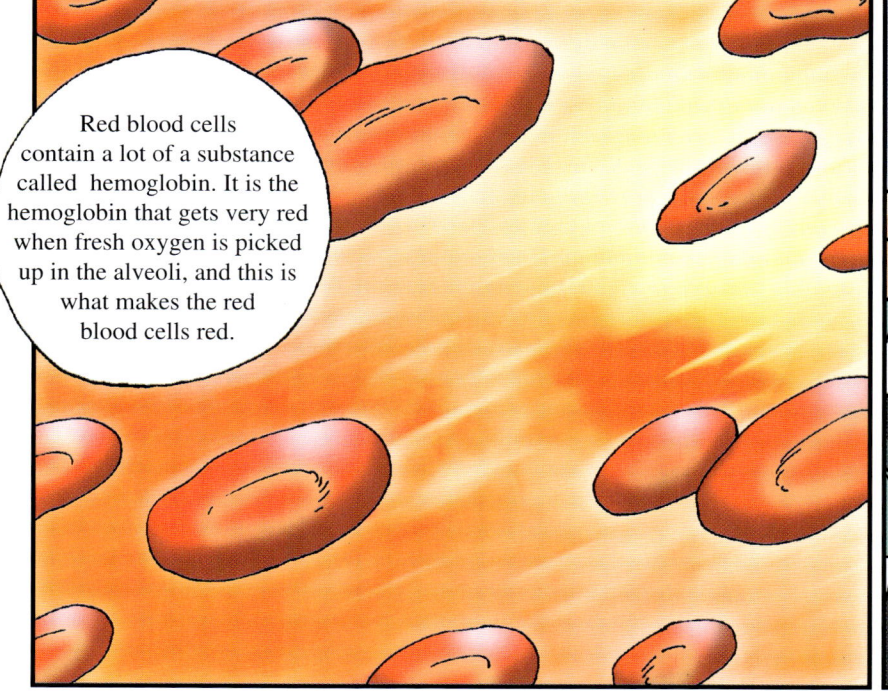

Those are red blood cells.

Red blood cells deliver fresh oxygen to the rest of our body.

Oh, I see...

But why are the red blood cells red?

Red blood cells contain a lot of a substance called hemoglobin. It is the hemoglobin that gets very red when fresh oxygen is picked up in the alveoli, and this is what makes the red blood cells red.

Look! That red blood cell is huge!

Yeah! You're right.

Ken, why are those red blood cells so big?

There are many different kinds of red blood cells.

Those just happen to be bigger.

Ahhhhh! It's... it's a fireball!!

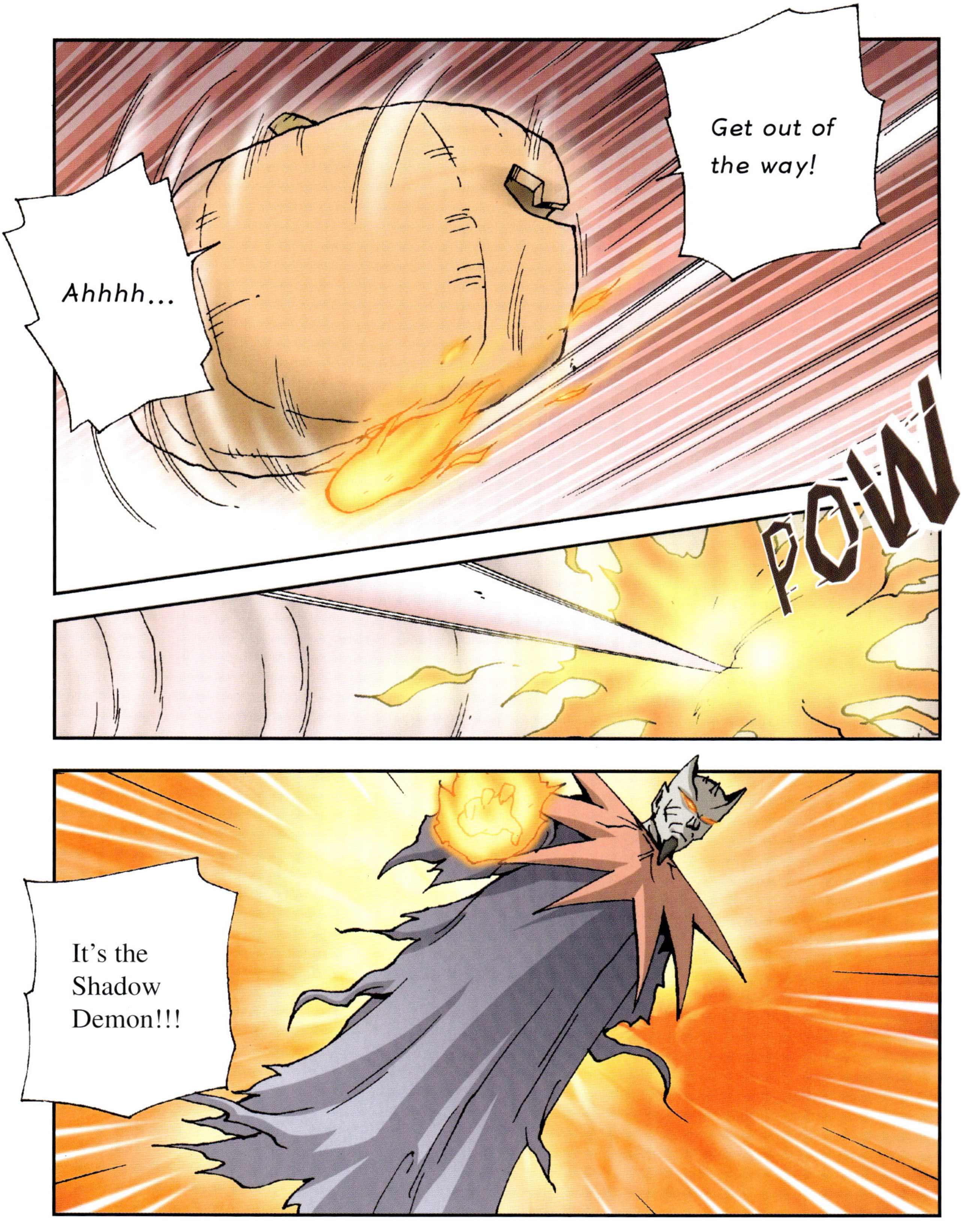
Get out of the way!
Ahhhh...
POW
It's the Shadow Demon!!!

Oh no! He's spotted us!

You haven't lost your touch, Romeo.

But now that I've seen you, it's the end of you!

I see you've sent a search party after me...

Hurry! Fire the net! Now!!!

102 A Journey into the Human Body

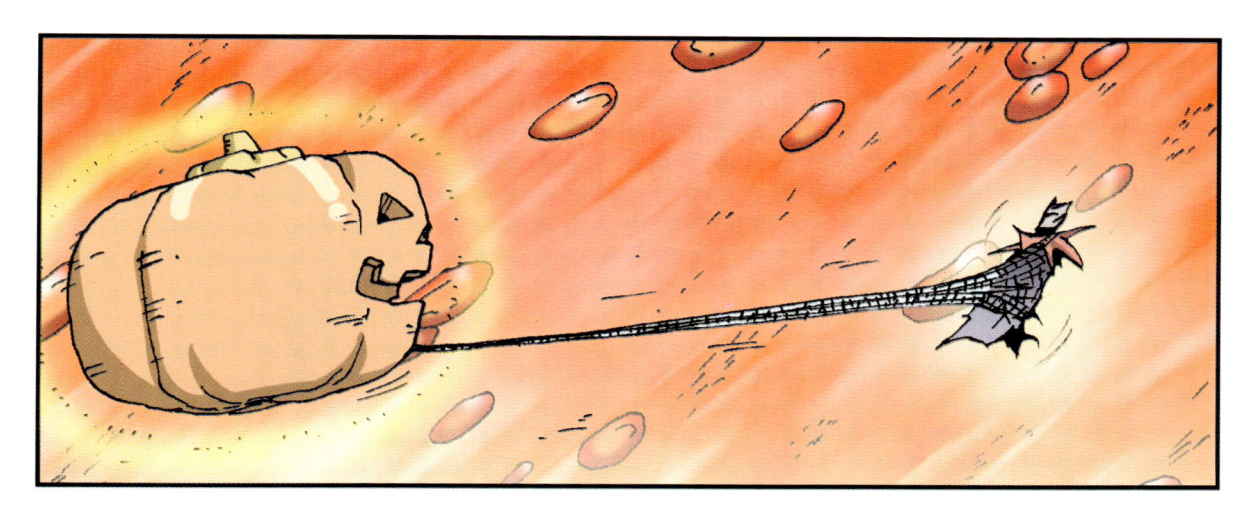

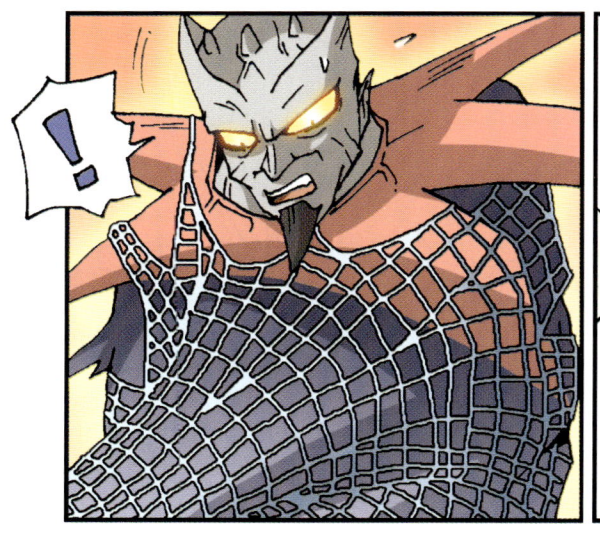

You think that's enough to stop the Shadow Demon?

This is nothing!!

!

Hehehe! That's not your ordinary king spider net, Shadow Demon!

That's five hundred king spider nets woven together by the fairies of Purple Land!

"Not even the White Dragon, who is stronger than you, can escape that!"

"W-what!!"

"Does that mean that we've caught the Shadow Demon??"

"Of course."

"I can't believe we caught him so easily."

"But I'm glad we did."

"Did you think you could catch me that easily?"

W-wait!! The demon is summoning another creature!!

What!! Oh my gosh!!

The Blood 105

Grrrrr–
SWOOSH
Ahhhh..!! It's Helldog! The dog that guards the gates of hell!!
Grooowwwl!!

Ahhhh! Gasp!!

I forgot about the Shadow Demon's summoning powers!!

We can't just sit here and let the dog destroy the submarine!!

But what can we do? We can't go outside!!

Retract the net. Let's get out of here!!

What!! You want us to release the Shadow Demon!!

Shoot! We had him, and now we have to let him go!!

So, you're going to run away...
Don't think I'll let you get away from me that easily.
Ahhhh... That beast won't let go!!
I'll destroy you all!!

Oh no!! We're finished.

What are we going to do now?

Hey, wait a minute!

!

They're attacking the Shadow Demon!

The Blood 109

White blood cells!!

White blood cells?

White blood cells attack bad, disease-causing substances that enter our bodies.

They think the demon is a disease!!

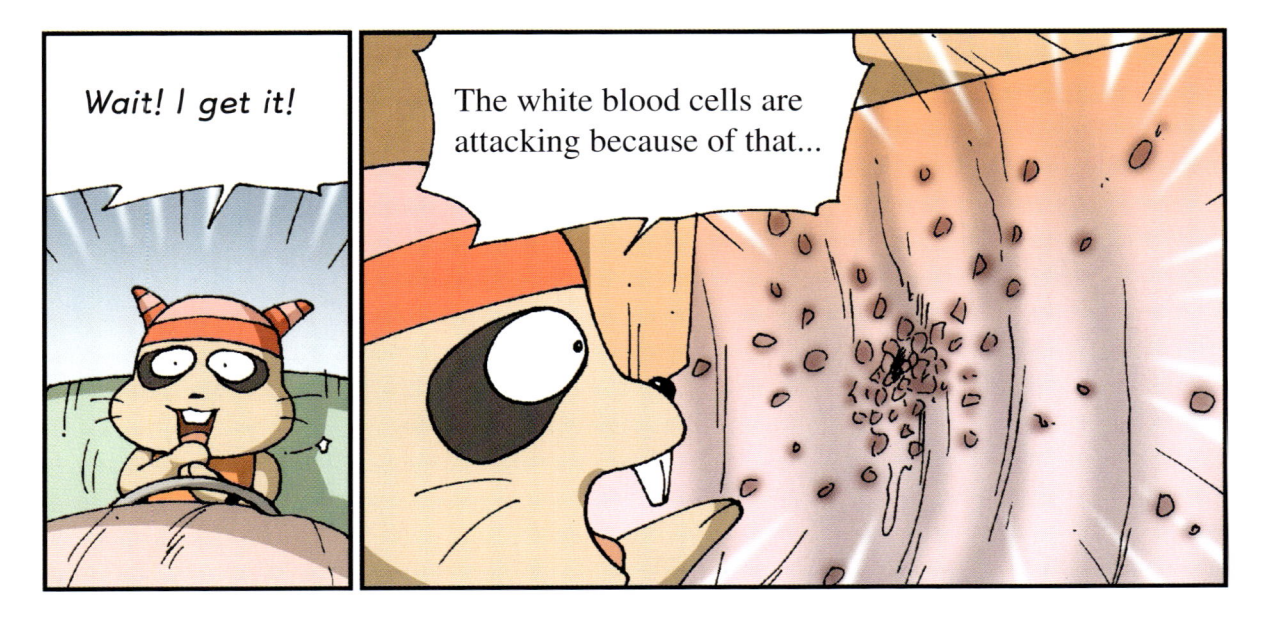

Helldog is under attack, too!

The white blood cells are attacking them both! Yeah...!!!

But how do they know who or what to attack?

Wait! I get it!

The white blood cells are attacking because of that...

The Blood

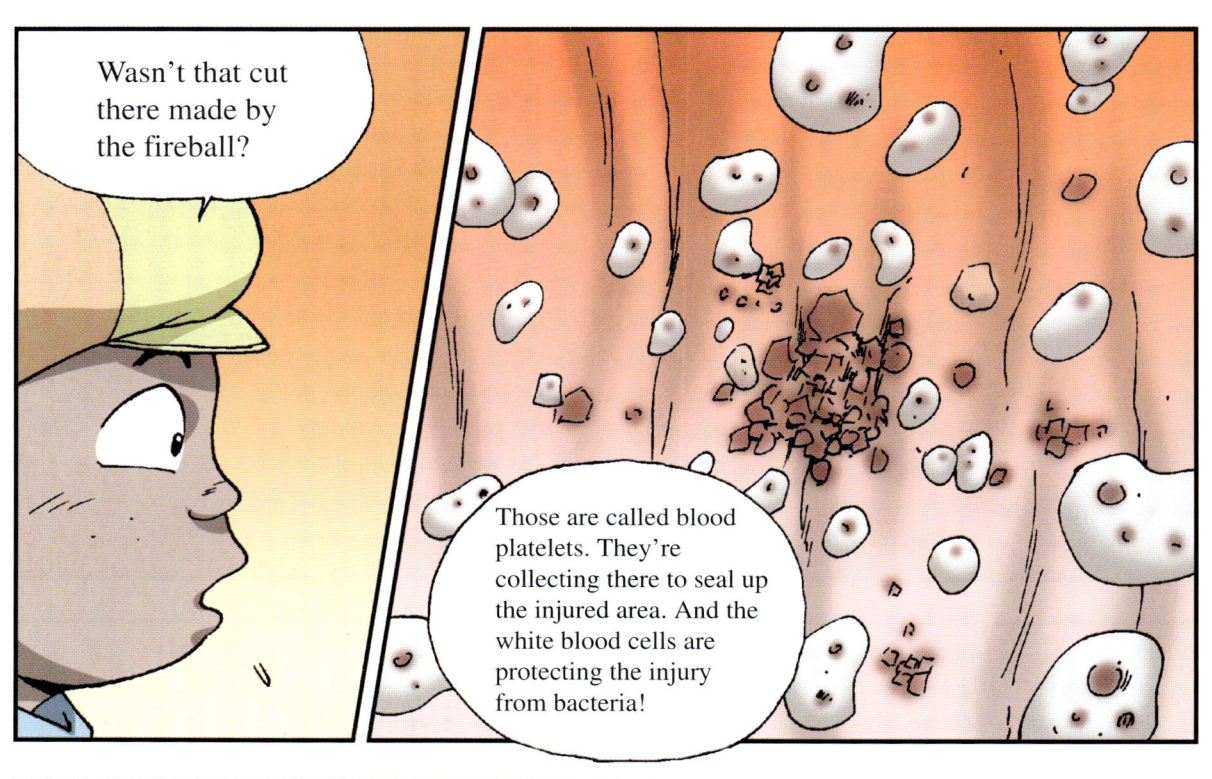

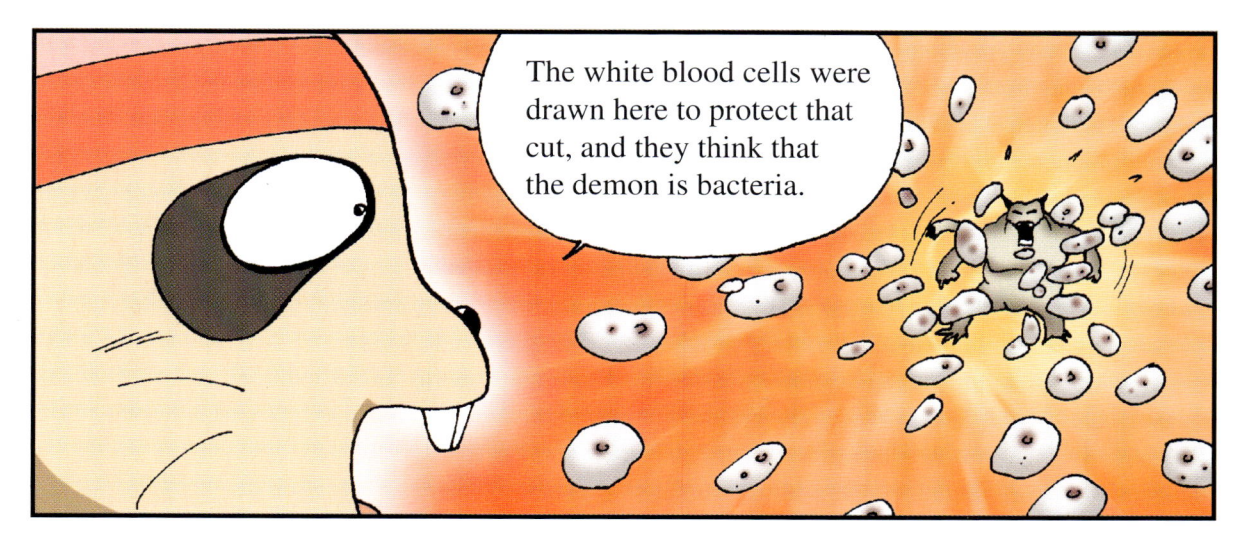

Wasn't that cut there made by the fireball?

Those are called blood platelets. They're collecting there to seal up the injured area. And the white blood cells are protecting the injury from bacteria!

Platelets. Oh, I see... The platelets are fixing the cut.

That's right.

The white blood cells were drawn here to protect that cut, and they think that the demon is bacteria.

112   A Journey into the Human Body

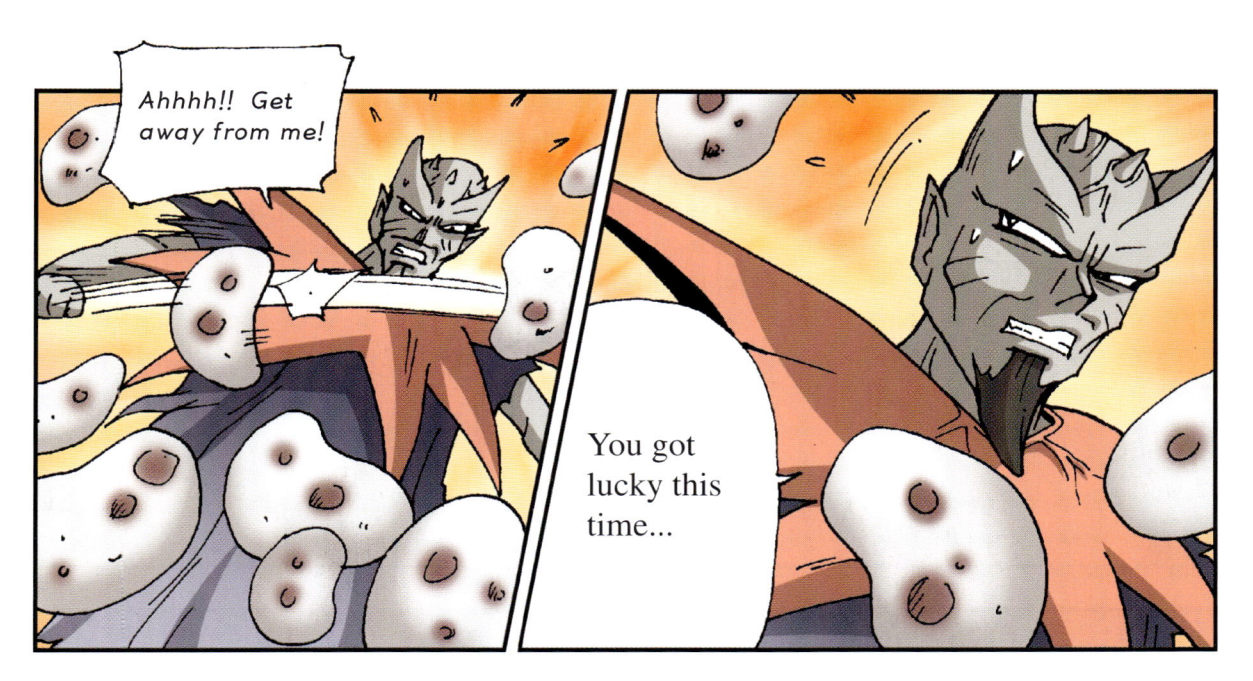

Ahhhh!! Get away from me!

You got lucky this time...

The Shadow Demon is disappearing again!!

I guess he couldn't stand the attack of the white blood cells!

He's gone!!

Whew— That was close...

The Blood 113

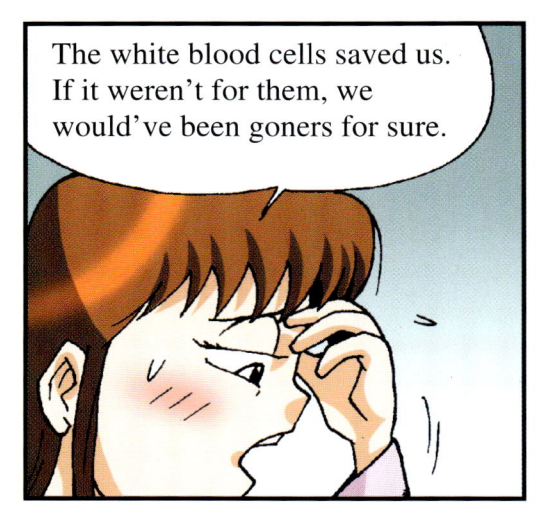

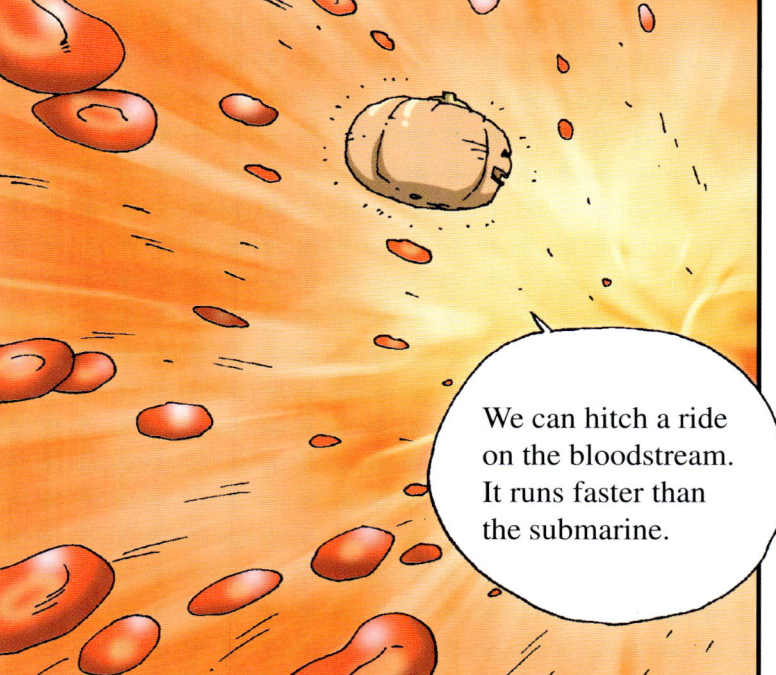

The white blood cells saved us. If it weren't for them, we would've been goners for sure.

Thanks!

Yeah! Me, too.

But, what now...? Even if we do catch the Shadow Demon again, how're we going to beat those creatures of his?

And our powers are no match for the Shadow Demon.

There is one way.

First things first. Let's get out of here. If we stay here any longer, the white blood cells will start attacking us.

We can hitch a ride on the bloodstream. It runs faster than the submarine.

How Blood Works

The blood is made up of white blood cells, red blood cells, and platelets.

White Blood Cells
These cells attack and gobble up foreign cells that enter our bodies.

Red Blood Cells
These cells are filled with hemoglobin, which has the very important task of transporting oxygen throughout our bodies. It is the hemoglobin that makes our blood look red.

Blood Platelets
These cells help blood to clot.

Blood is not just a red liquid we have in our bodies. It contains many, many different things. Blood travels throughout our body delivering oxygen and nutrients, but blood also has many other important functions.

The Blood 115

Veins and Arteries

Blood is red, so why are the veins on our arms blue?

See? Shouldn't they be red?

You're right.

Why is that, Ken? Is it because of the skin?

No, not exactly.

116 A Journey into the Human Body

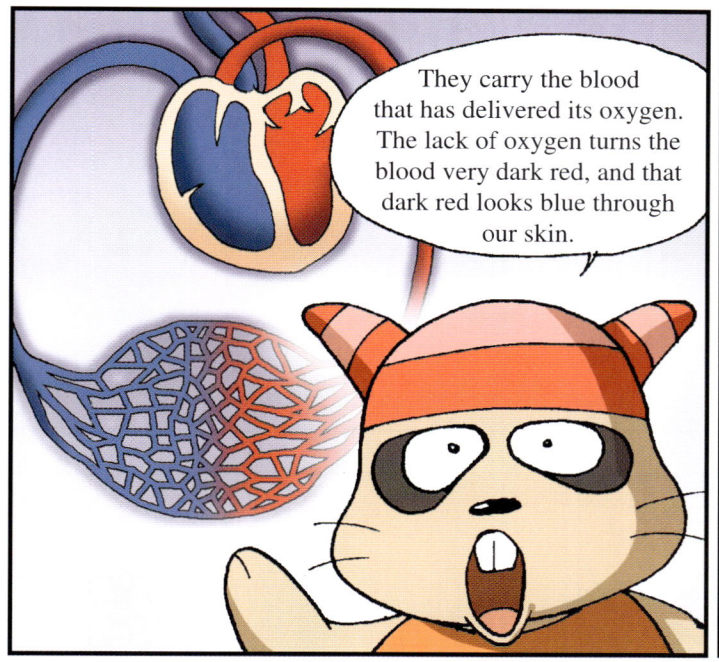

The blood vessels you see in your arms are called veins.

Veins?

They carry the blood that has delivered its oxygen. The lack of oxygen turns the blood very dark red, and that dark red looks blue through our skin.

Oh...I didn't know that blood without oxygen traveled through our body.

Now the blood here is a bright red. Why is that?

That's because we are traveling through an artery, not a vein.

Veins and Arteries **117**

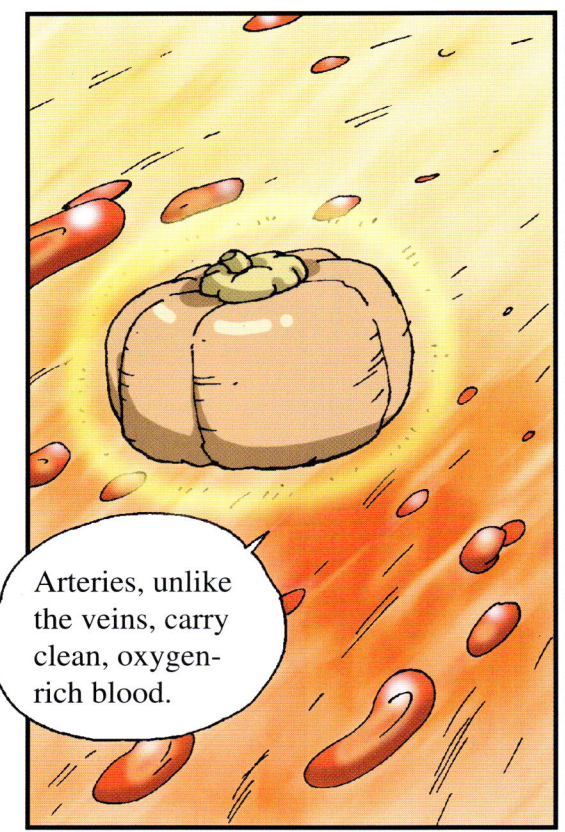

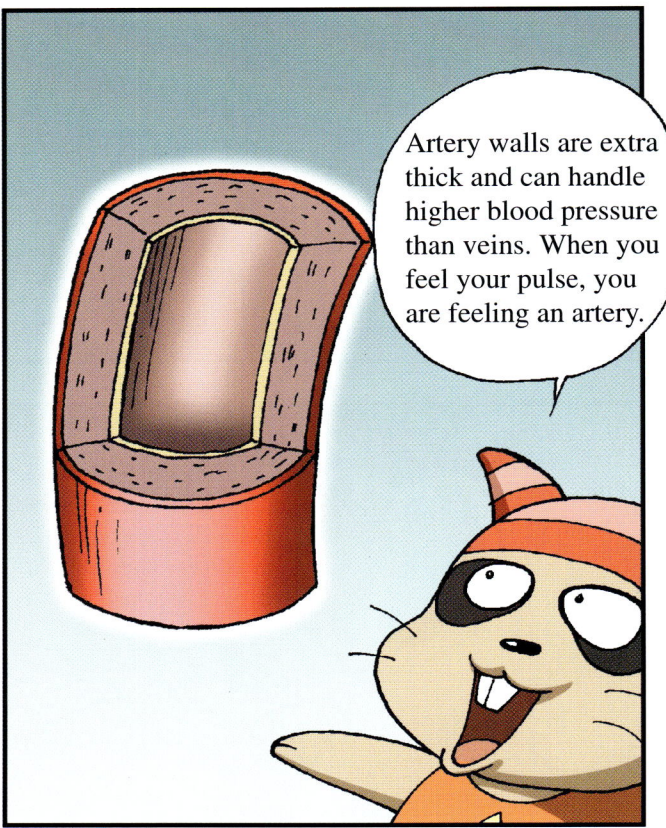

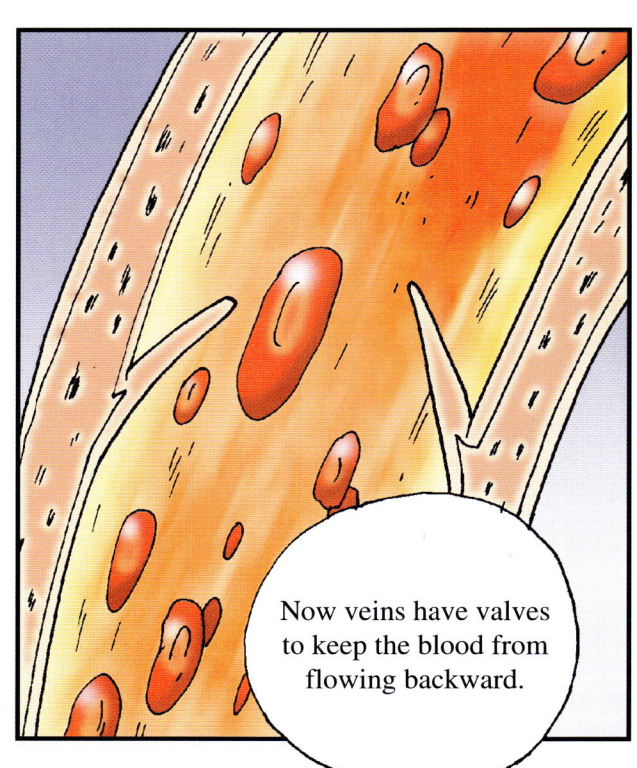

Arteries, unlike the veins, carry clean, oxygen-rich blood.

Artery walls are extra thick and can handle higher blood pressure than veins. When you feel your pulse, you are feeling an artery.

Now veins have valves to keep the blood from flowing backward.

Can blood really flow backwards...?

Yes...

118   A Journey into the Human Body

...but if it does, then we're in big trouble. That's why we have venous valves.

Wow— The body is just full of wonderful and surprising things...

It's great how blood travels all over the body delivering nutrients and oxygen.

And then the blood cells head back to the heart and lungs again for more oxygen. This is called circulation.

Ken, what are capillaries?

Veins and Arteries 119

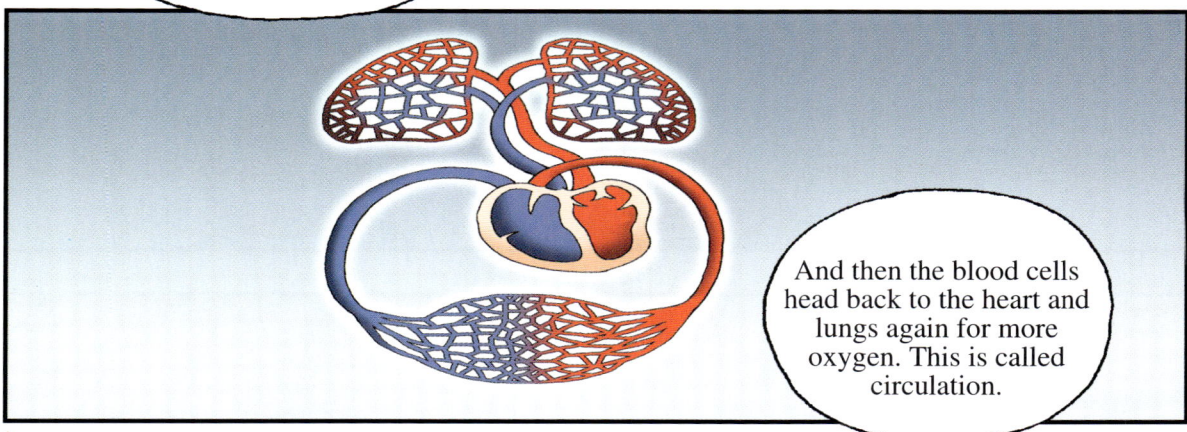

Capillaries are very thin blood vessels.

Only one red blood cell at a time can pass through a capillary.

But what do capillaries do?

Capillaries deliver oxygen to areas where the thicker arteries can't go.

120 A Journey into the Human Body

I never knew that the human body was so well organized!

Now you know, thanks to me.

So what was your idea for catching the Shadow Demon?

Yes, tell us Ken.

Well, all we have to do is stop the Shadow Demon from summoning his creatures.

What? You're going to stop him from what?

How??

Veins and Arteries 121

How Blood Vessels Work

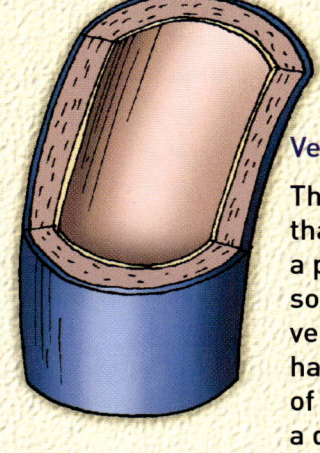

Veins

The veins have thinner walls than the arteries. Veins do not have a pulse. Blood in the veins could sometimes flow backwards, but the venous valves prevent that from happening. Blood in the veins is full of carbon dioxide, which is why it's a dark shade of red.

Veins are blood vessels that carry blood back to the heart.

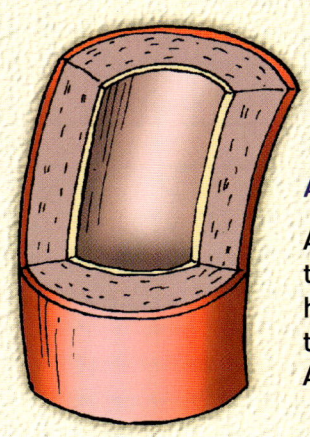

Arteries

Arteries are blood vessels that transport blood away from the heart. Artery walls are thicker and tougher than the walls of veins. Arteries have a pulse.

Arterial blood is rich in oxygen, which is why it is bright red.

Capillaries

Capillary walls are made up of a single layer of cells and are very thin. Only one red blood cell at a time can pass through capillaries. The walls are so thin that water, carbon dioxide, and oxygen can pass through them freely.

122   A Journey into the Human Body

After the blood travels throughout our bodies, it picks up more oxygen in the lungs.

Lungs

Arteries

Heart

Veins

Capillaries

The blood leaves the heart, and the arteries and capillaries carry the oxygen to all parts of our bodies.

Veins and Arteries

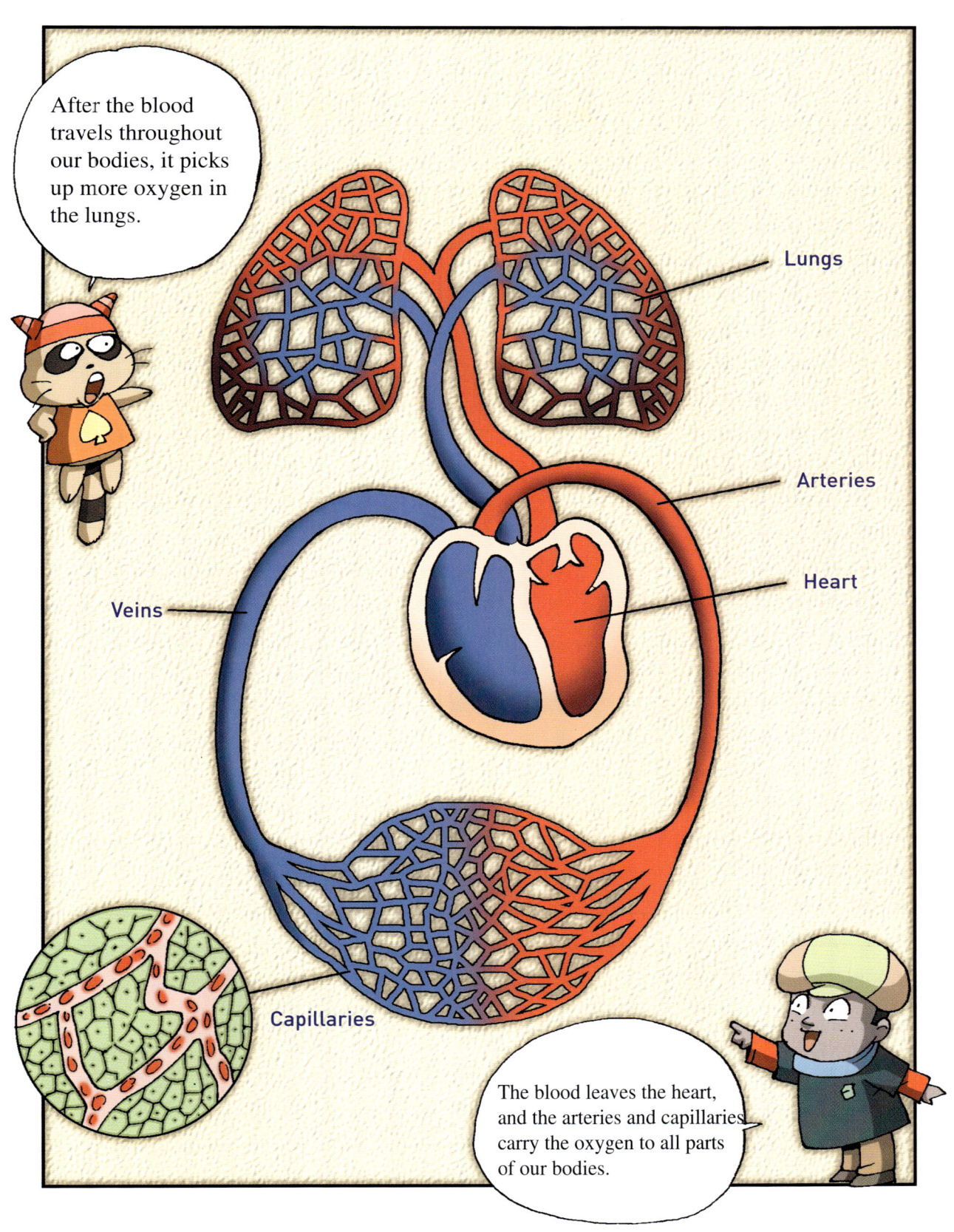

The Heart

I was watching the Shadow Demon earlier and noticed that the spell he uses to summon creatures from another world is a rather long one.

Ken, please explain your plan.

Not only that, he's got to concentrate until the creature takes shape completely.

Get it! So you're saying that one of us should distract the Shadow Demon so that he can't summon a creature, right?

That's right!

While one of you distracts him, someone else should lead him to Colossical.

But who's going to do that? It sounds really dangerous!

It looks like you're the man for the job, Ken.

W-what !!

I'm the greatest treasure in the wizard world! You should be protecting me, not throwing me to the wolves!!

See? That's it, Ken!? That's how you should distract the Shadow Demon! With your big mouth... hahahaha!

The Heart 125

Swooosh—

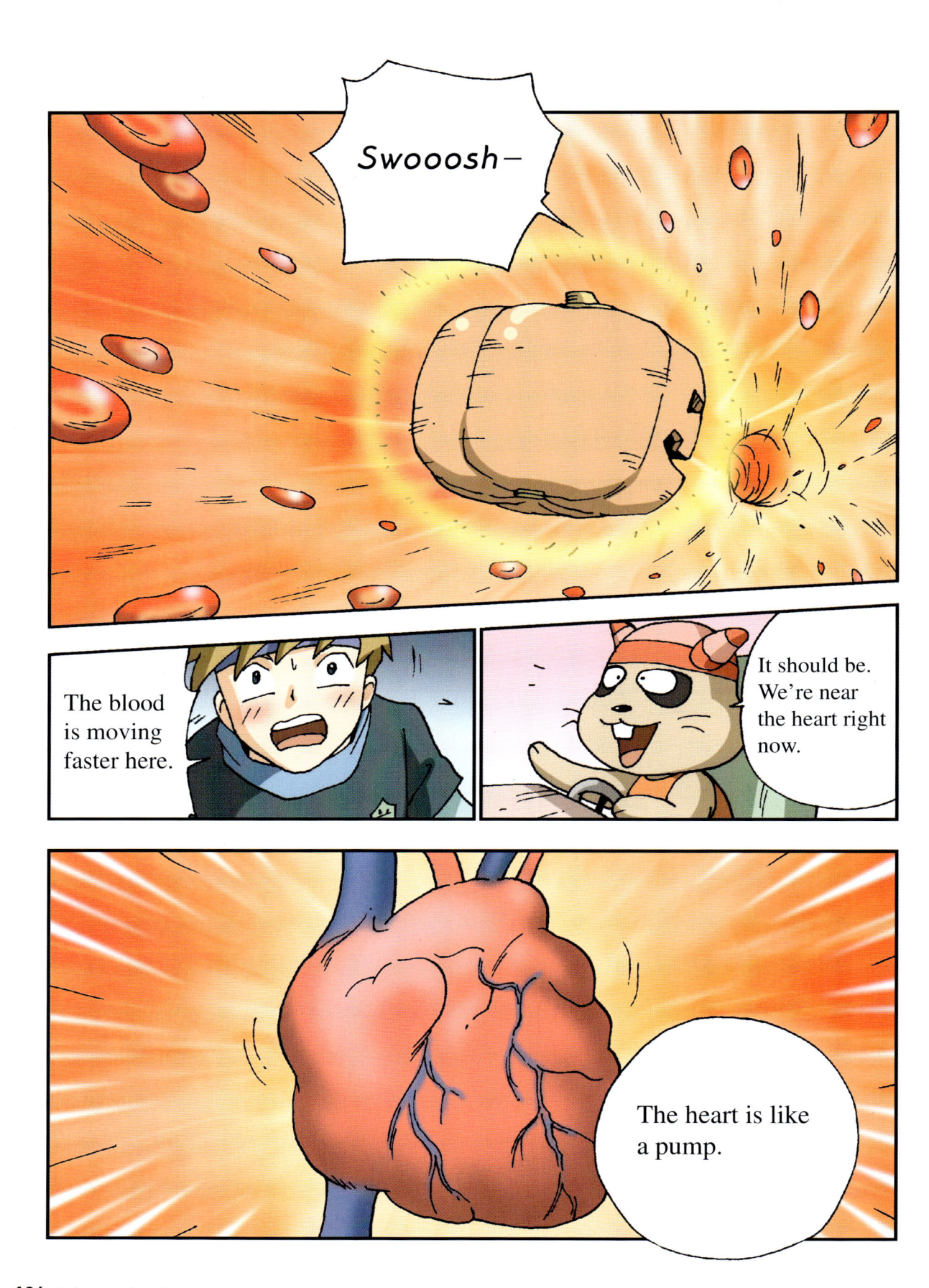

The blood is moving faster here.

It should be. We're near the heart right now.

The heart is like a pump.

The heart is about the size of your fist and is made up of muscle pockets, or chambers.

The heart pushes blood throughout the body.

As the heart contracts and gets smaller, it sends blood out into the arteries.

When the heart relaxes and expands, it sucks in blood from the veins.

The Heart

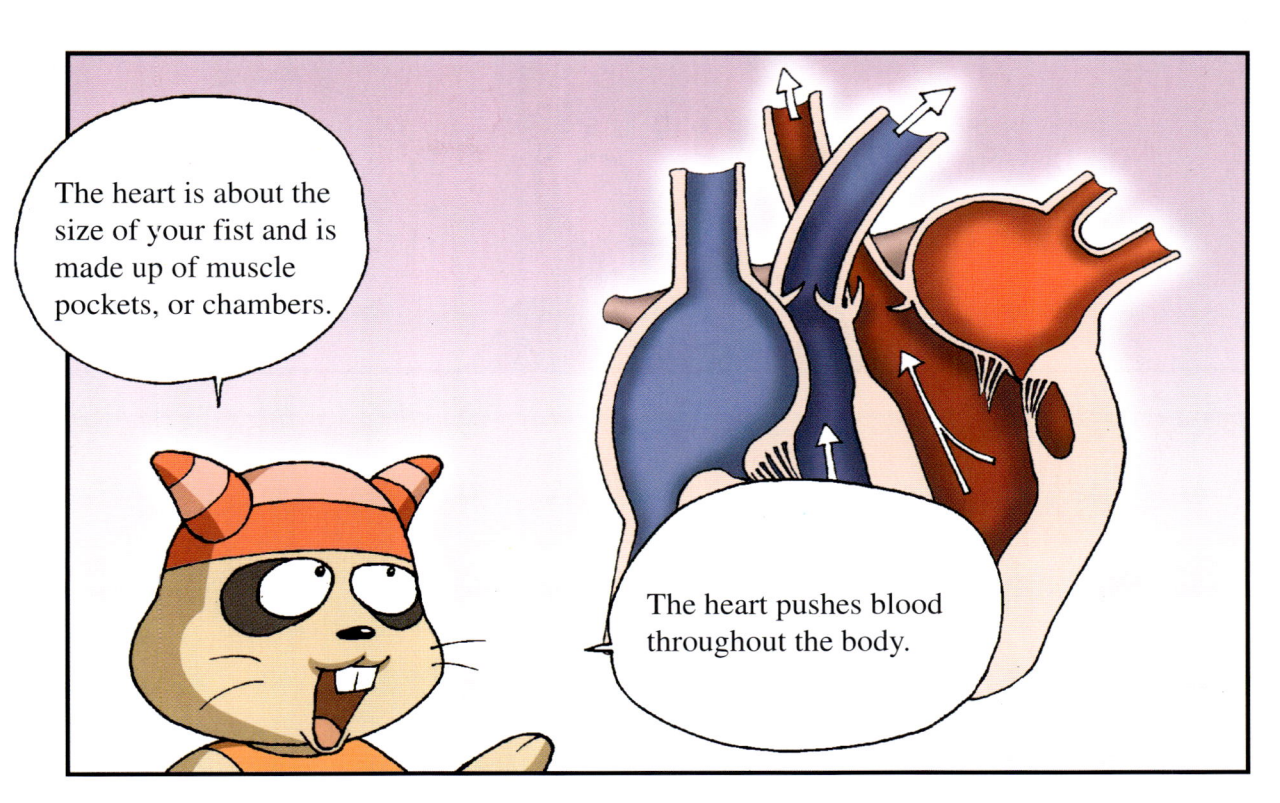

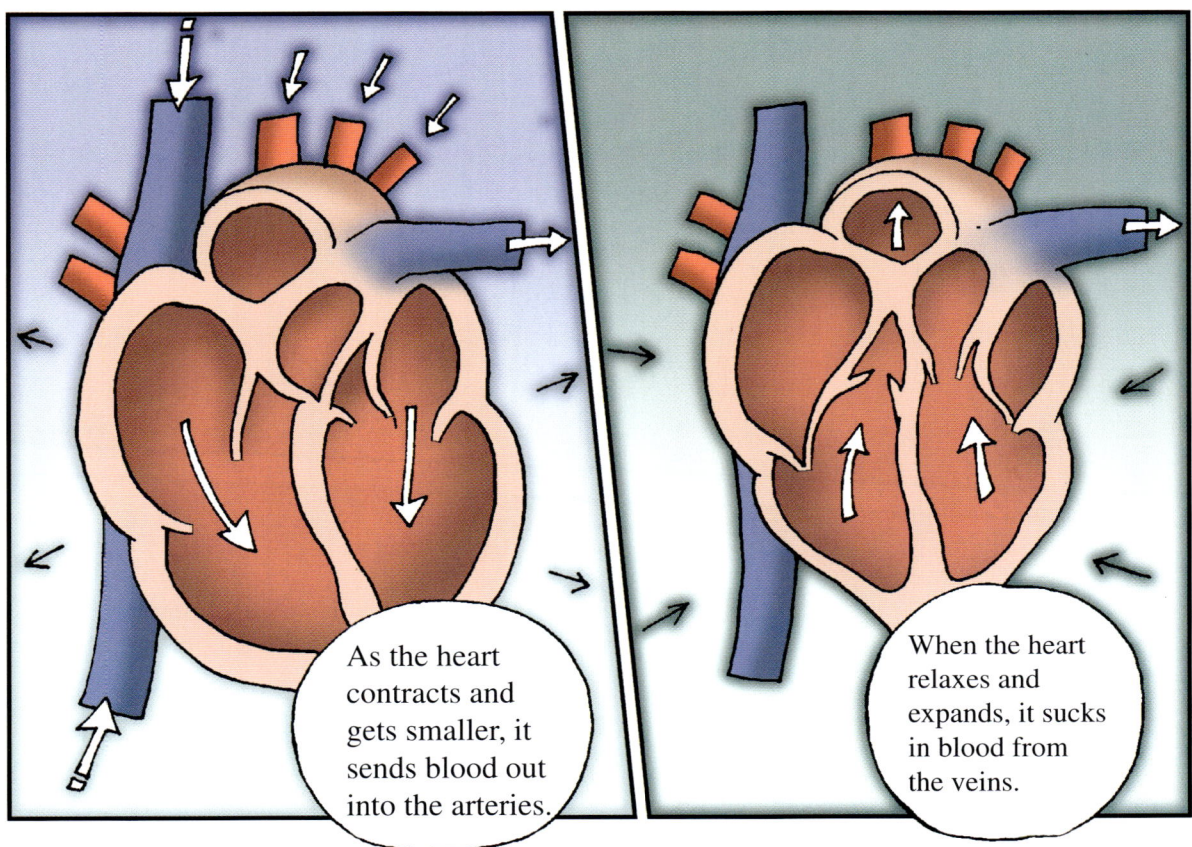

So that's how the blood circulates around our body!

What's going on?!

That's the heartbeat.

We're about to enter the heart. It'll be like riding a roller coaster.

Uh...I don't like roller coasters.

Hehehe... Well, I love 'em! I could ride 'em all day!

We'll see about that!

Ahhhhhh!!! Oooomph!

The Heart 129

130 A Journey into the Human Body

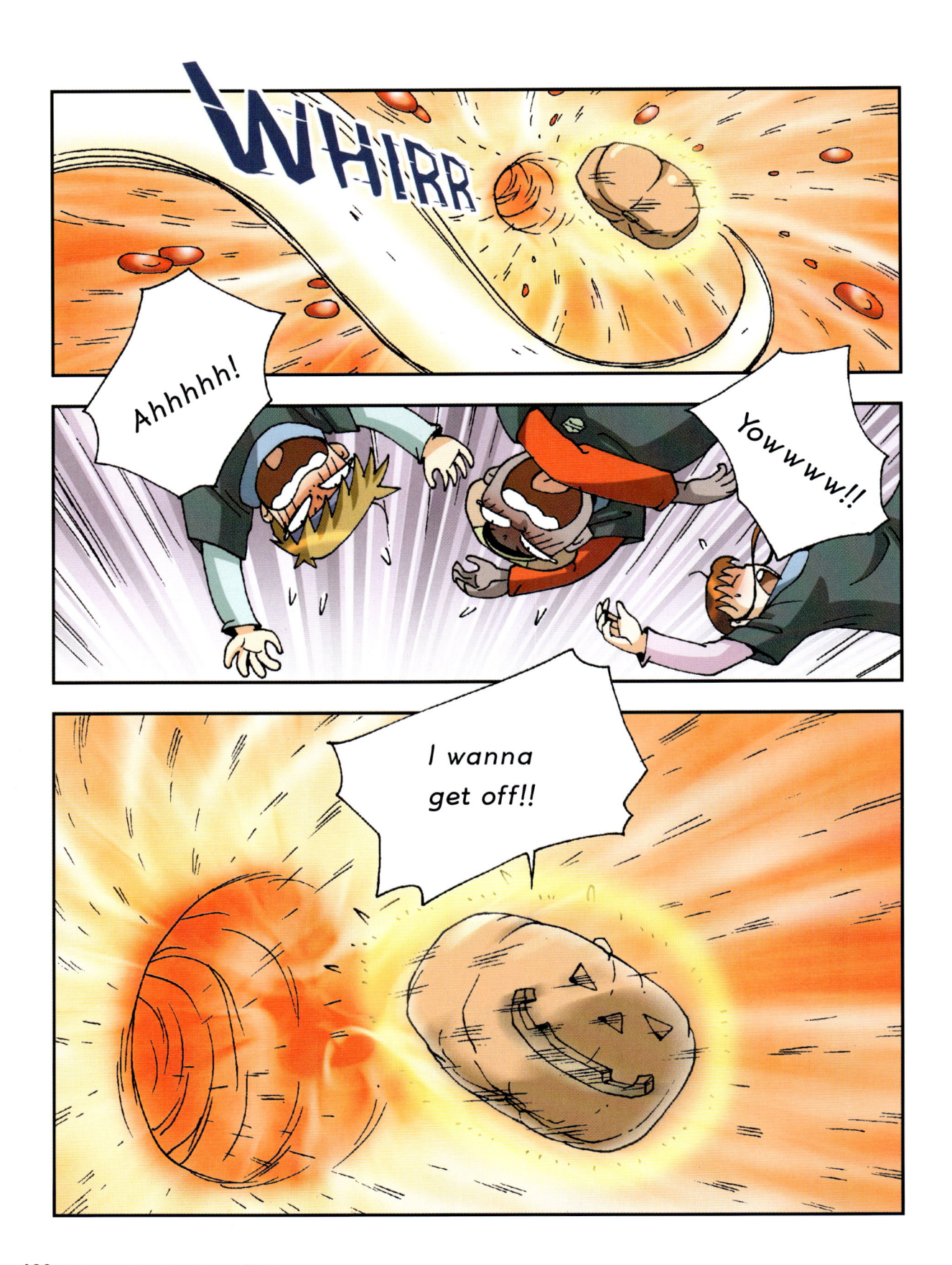

Noooo! We're falling!!

WHIRR

Oh— I'm so dizzy...

Finally, we've made it to the powerhouse of the body... the heart!

So, we're inside the heart now?

Yes. We're in the right atrium now.

The Heart 131

The heartbeat sounds like a very loud drum.

Do you know how many times the heart beats in a day?

Hmmm... no...

It beats 100,800 times in a single day!

And it circulates about eight thousand liters of blood a day.

Really? It beats that many times?!!

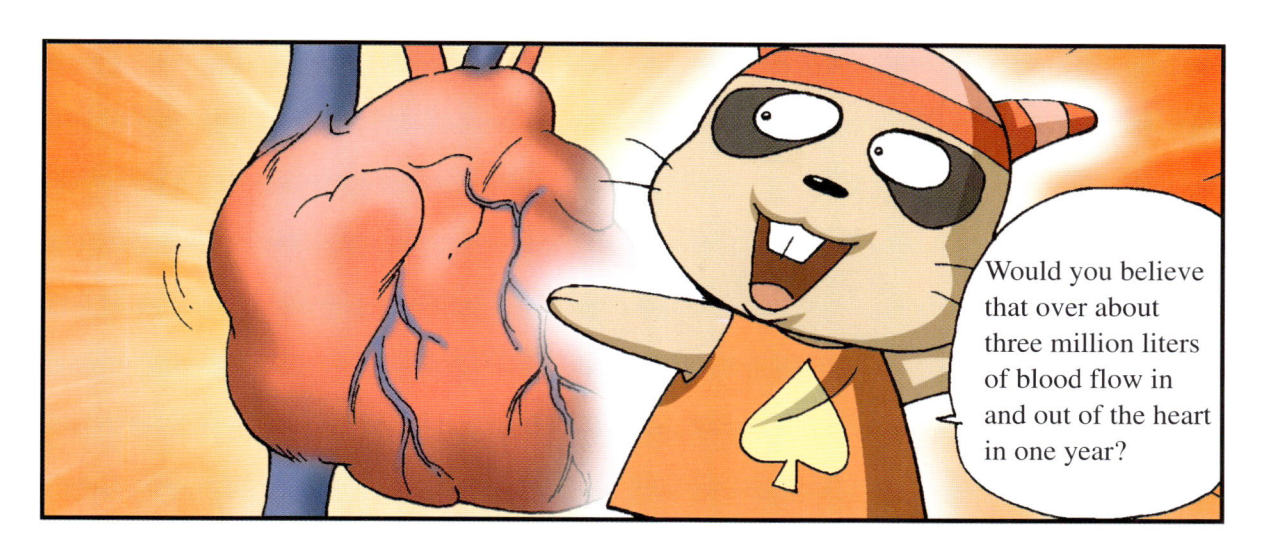

Would you believe that over about three million liters of blood flow in and out of the heart in one year?

Three million liters? That's enough to fill several swimming pools.

Yup...

The heart is a strong muscle, and pumping out that much blood in one day is a cinch.

I knew that the heart was important, but I didn't know it did that much work...

Do you know which part of the body receives the most blood?

The Heart 133

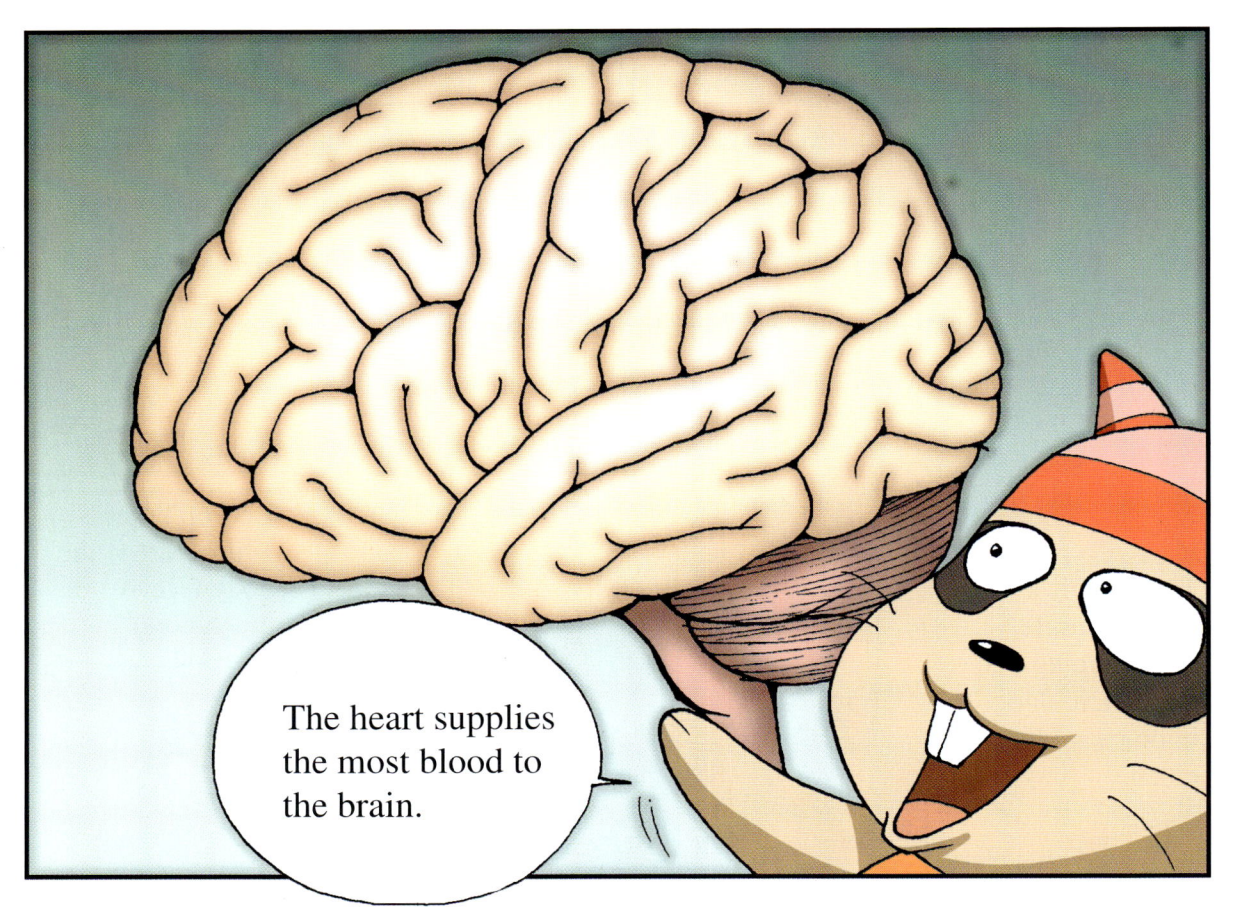

Maybe the stomach... After all, the stomach continues to digest food even while we sleep.

I think it's the lungs... The stomach at least gets to rest once in a while, but the lungs work twenty-four hours a day!

You're both wrong.

What!! So what's the answer?

The heart supplies the most blood to the brain.

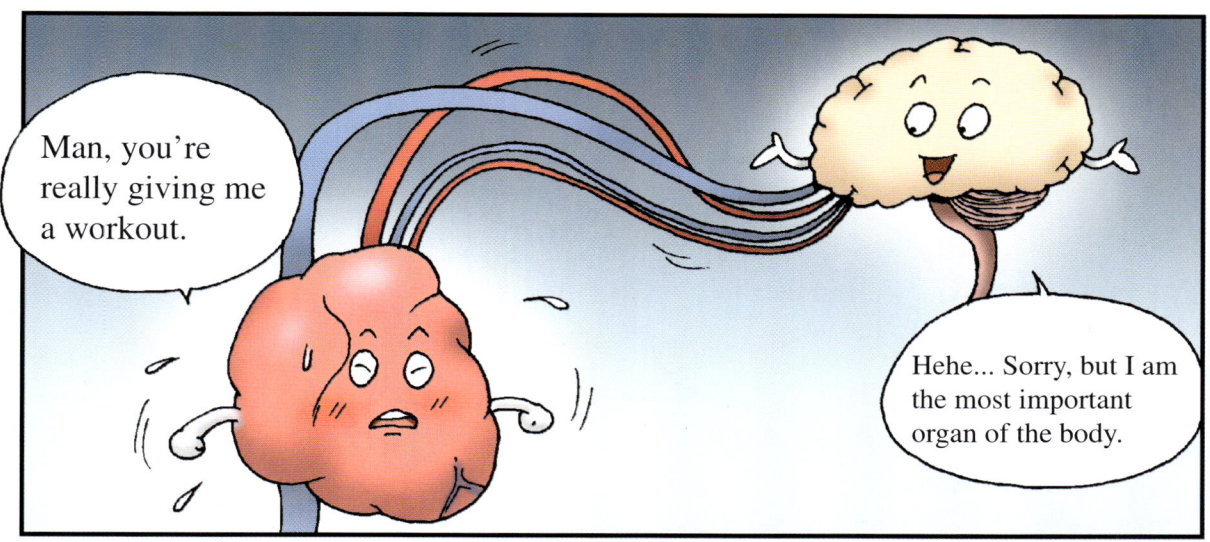

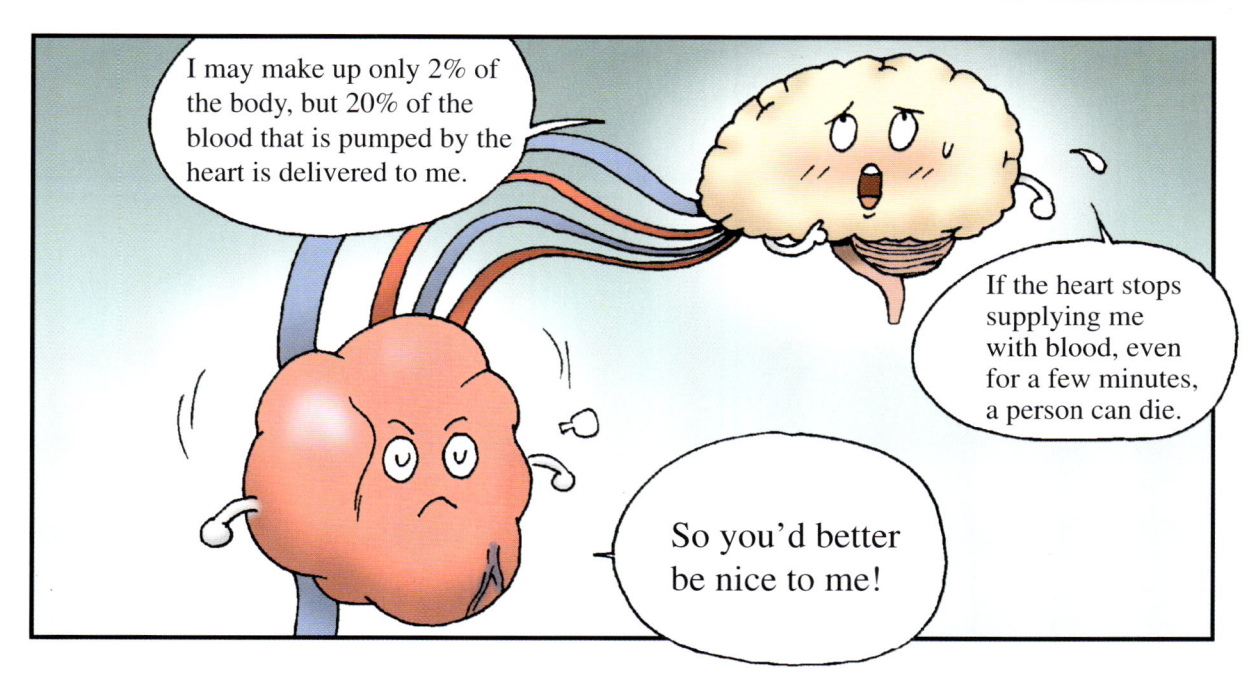

The brain!!

But the brain doesn't move!!

Man, you're really giving me a workout.

Hehe... Sorry, but I am the most important organ of the body.

I may make up only 2% of the body, but 20% of the blood that is pumped by the heart is delivered to me.

If the heart stops supplying me with blood, even for a few minutes, a person can die.

So you'd better be nice to me!

Okay, now let's move up into the next chamber.
Blood flows through the vena cava to the right atrium, then to the right ventricle...
...and then to the lungs.
Then it goes through the pulmonary vein to the left atrium and left ventricle and then out into the body.
Whoa— How'd you know that?
My grandma's had heart surgery twice...

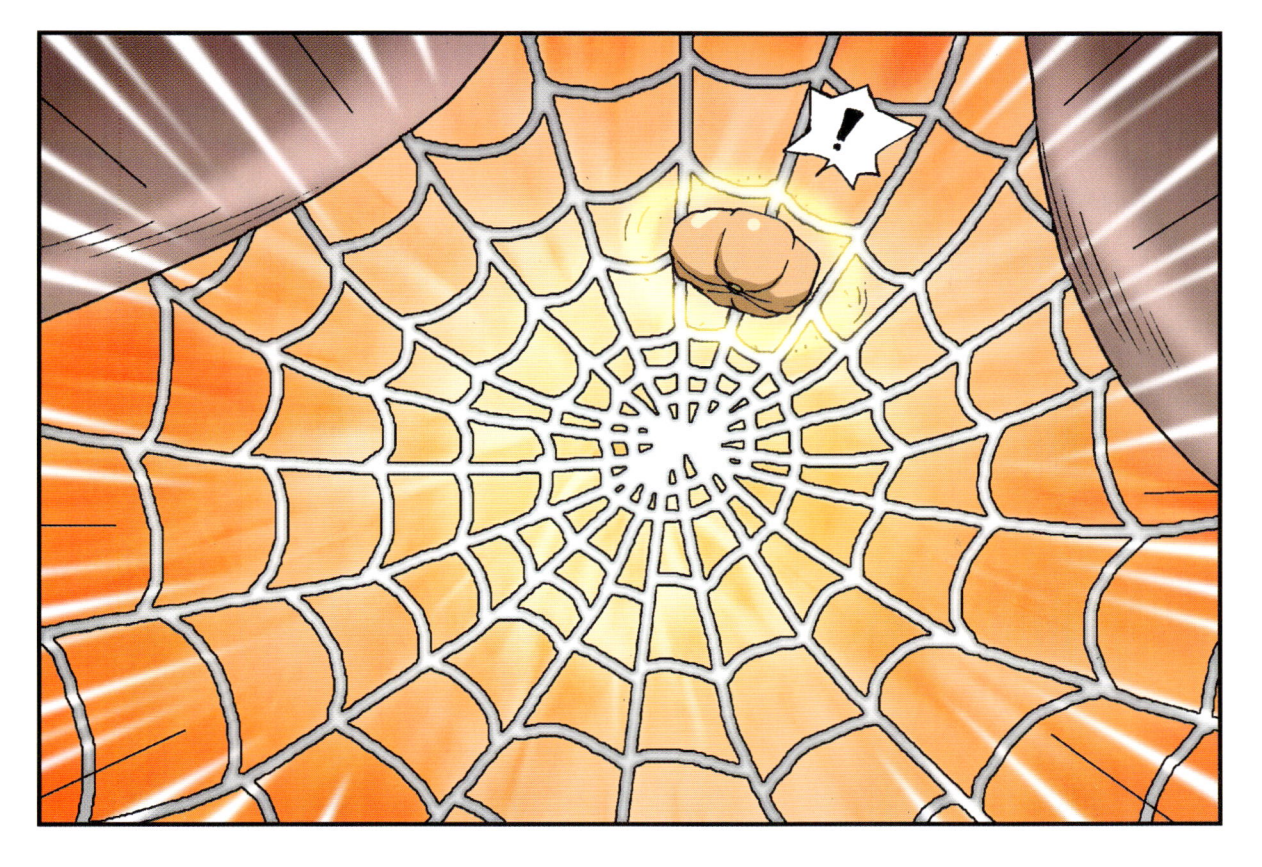

BANG

Ooommph!

W-what is that !!

!

Oh my gosh! It's a spider web!!

Why is there a spider web inside the heart?!!

I think this is the Shadow Demon's doing.

Let's get out of here!

Okay.

CREEK

CREEK

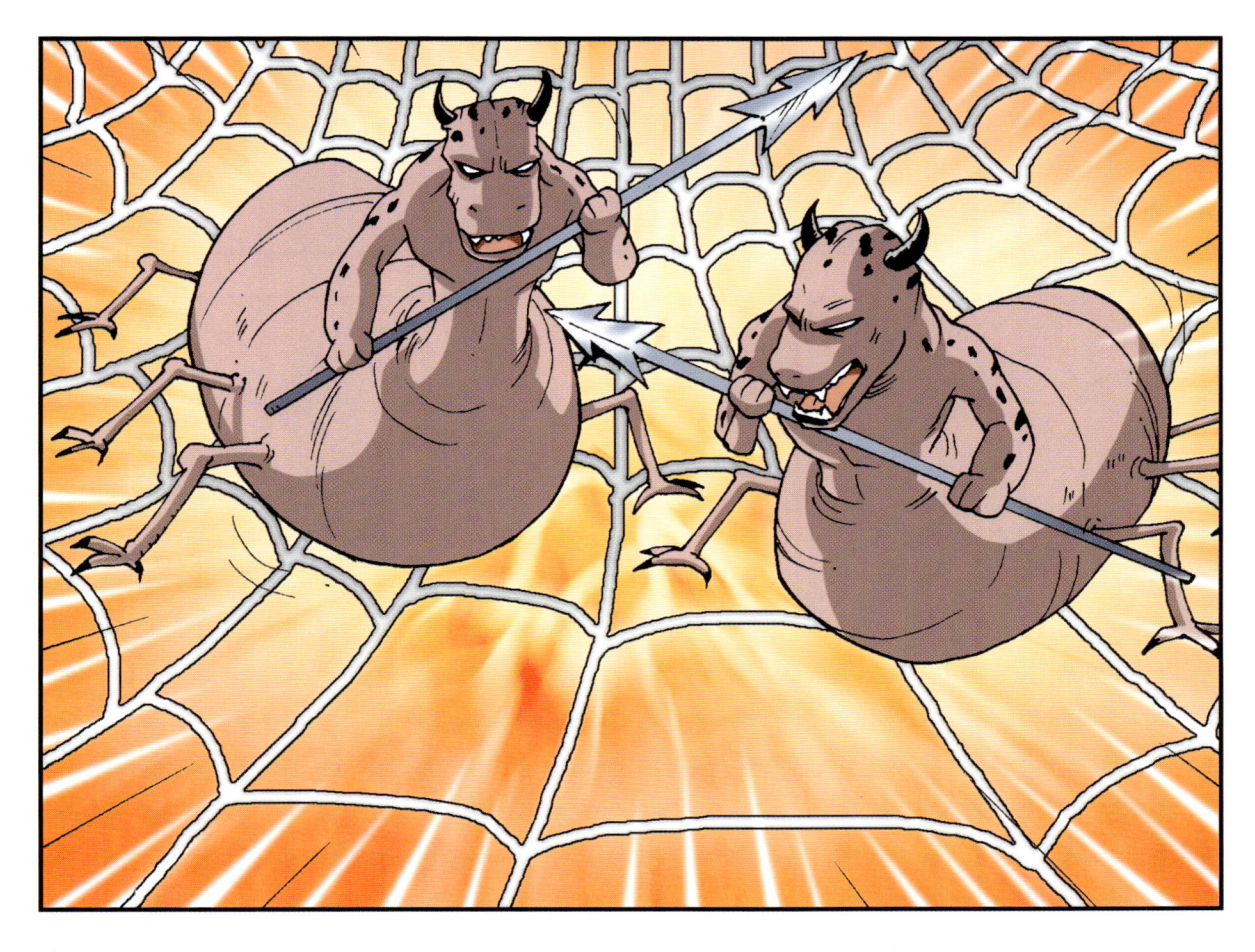

Argh... It won't come free.

Give it more gas!!

It's not working. I'm afraid if I give it more gas, the engine'll explode...

Oh my gosh! L-look!

The Heart **139**

Oh no...!!

I've never seen anything like that in my life! What the heck are those things!!

Those are vampire spiders!!

Vampire spiders...!!

Vampire spiders are incredibly strong and powerful.

BAM

BAM

140 A Journey into the Human Body

Ken! What are we going to do!! I can't move the submarine!

Spiders are afraid of fire... We can use fire!

Fire?? Does the submarine have a flamethrower?

Actually, no...

So then what are we going to do !! We can't use fire magic..

Even if we could, our fire magic isn't strong enough.

BAM

BAM

The Heart 141

"They're going to wreck this submarine!"

"Oh... please!"

"How are we going to handle them?"

"Y-yeah... that's it..."

"What's your idea?"

"Joon, how far have you gotten on the boundary spells?"

"Just to level two..."

"What about you, Yuna?"

"Level three."

"Good, me too."

"That should be enough."

"We'll have to go outside."

"You want to use the boundary spell in here?"

"That'll set this whole submarine on fire!"

What!!??

The Heart

Hurry up! We can't just sit here!

Let's go outside!

BAM
BAM

If the spiders see us, we're dead!

Be careful, you guys...

144 A Journey into the Human Body

All right. Everyone hold hands.

On three, we say the magic words.

Okay!

One! Two! Three!

ㅎㅍㅌ ㄹㅅㅂ ...

The Heart 145

Tssst—
Tsst—

146 A Journey into the Human Body

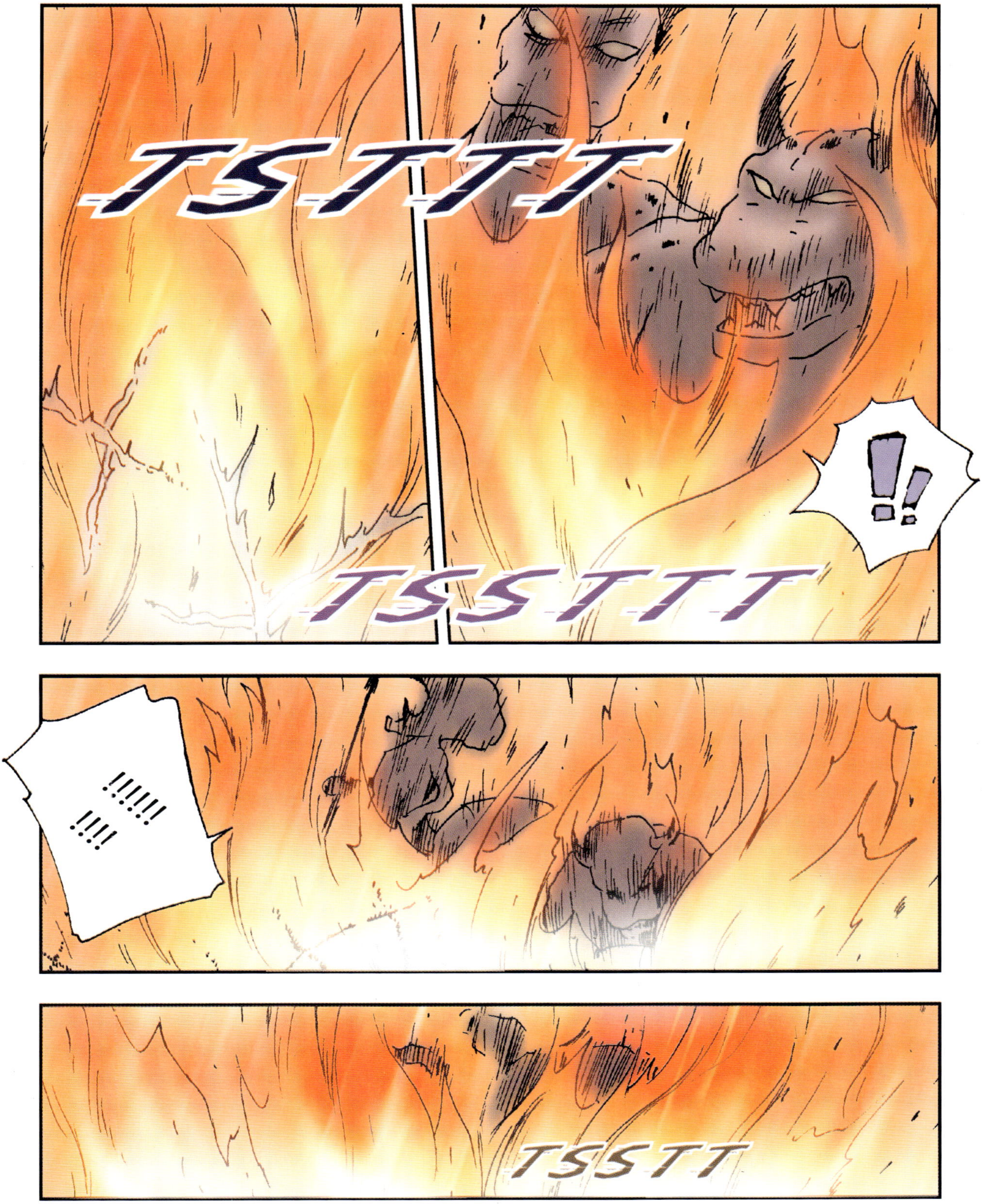

TSTTT
!!
TSSTTT
TSSTT

We did it...!!

The fire worked!

We had the element of surprise on our side.

Hehehe! Good job! You guys are awesome!!

Let's get out of here. We're in trouble if the Shadow Demon decides to show up.

Let's get back inside!

WHIRR

I think the Shadow Demon knew we were coming and summoned those creatures to head us off.

But I wonder why the Shadow Demon wasn't there, too.

I don't know. If he had been there, we would've been in big trouble.

He's up to something. I just know it!

What do you mean?

The Heart

"I think he sent those creatures to distract us and buy himself some time..."

"Yeah. That's the only reasonable explanation for why he didn't show up back there."

"This is beginning to freak me out. I don't want to see what he's got planned for us."

"Worries only bring on more worries, you know. Be brave."

"After all, you do have the all-powerful Ken on your side!"

"Fine. We won't know what lies ahead until we get there."

"But where are we going?"

"We're on our way to the kidneys."

How the Heart Works

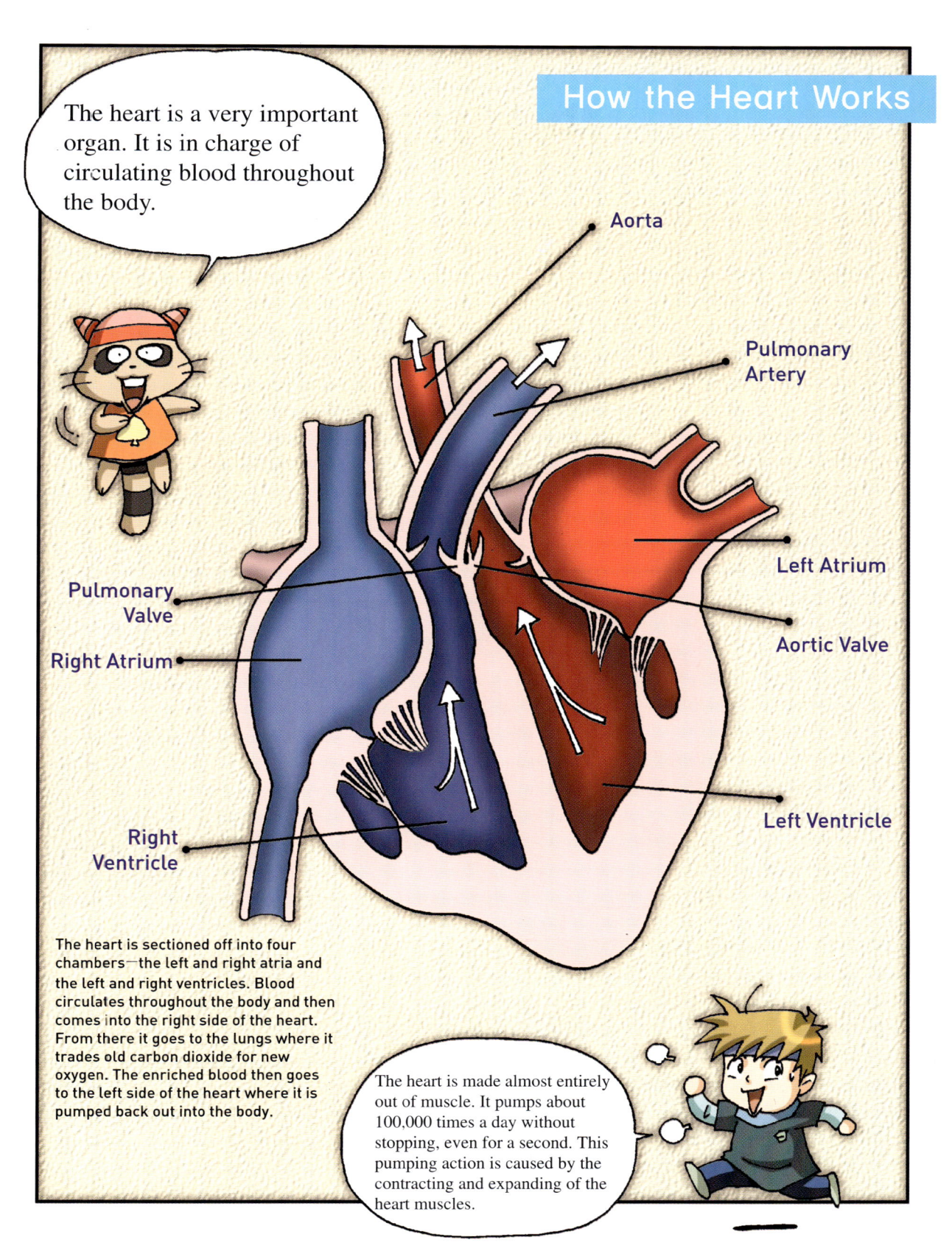

The heart is a very important organ. It is in charge of circulating blood throughout the body.

- Aorta
- Pulmonary Artery
- Left Atrium
- Aortic Valve
- Left Ventricle
- Pulmonary Valve
- Right Atrium
- Right Ventricle

The heart is sectioned off into four chambers—the left and right atria and the left and right ventricles. Blood circulates throughout the body and then comes into the right side of the heart. From there it goes to the lungs where it trades old carbon dioxide for new oxygen. The enriched blood then goes to the left side of the heart where it is pumped back out into the body.

The heart is made almost entirely out of muscle. It pumps about 100,000 times a day without stopping, even for a second. This pumping action is caused by the contracting and expanding of the heart muscles.

The Heart

The Kidneys

The Shadow Demon's gone from the radar.

What!! Where did he go??

Let's just stick to our plan and look through the kidneys.

Okay.

152   A Journey into the Human Body

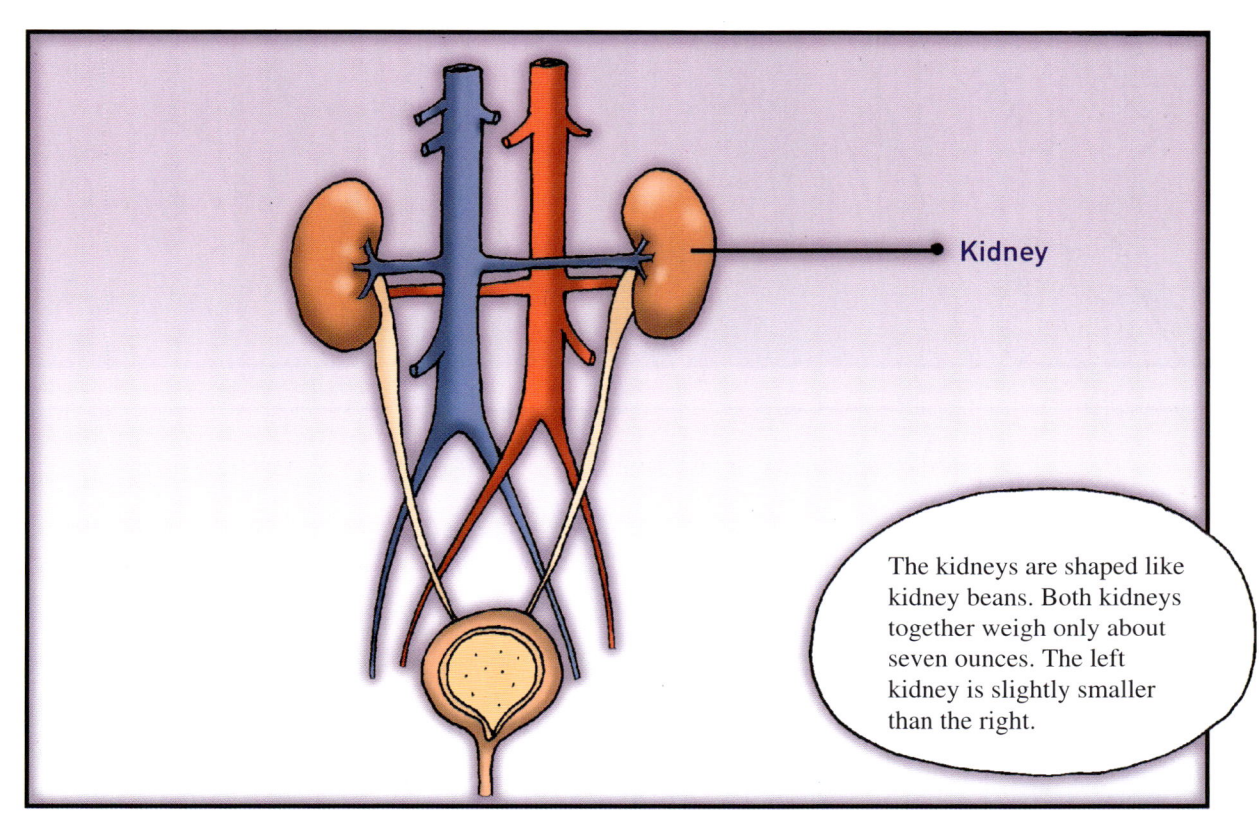

Wow— The kidneys are cool, too!

The kidneys are the body's filters. They filter out everything in the blood that the body doesn't need, and they help balance the amount of water that stays in the body.

Kidney

The kidneys are shaped like kidney beans. Both kidneys together weigh only about seven ounces. The left kidney is slightly smaller than the right.

The Kidneys   153

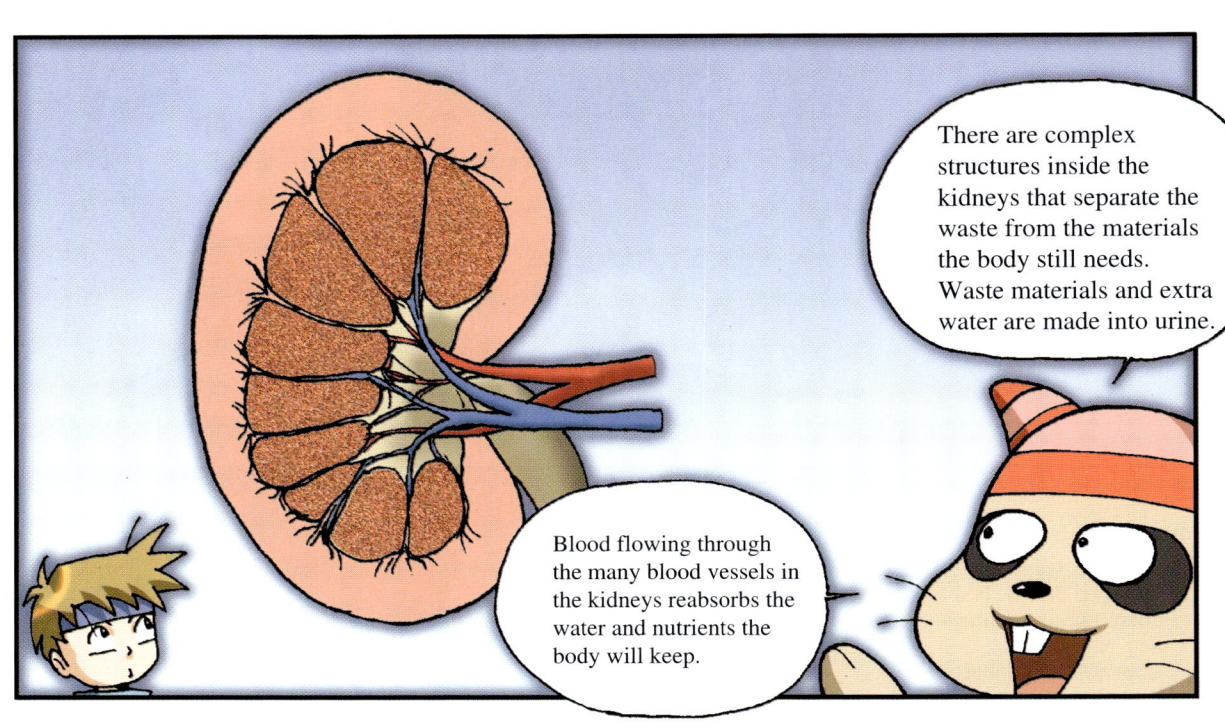

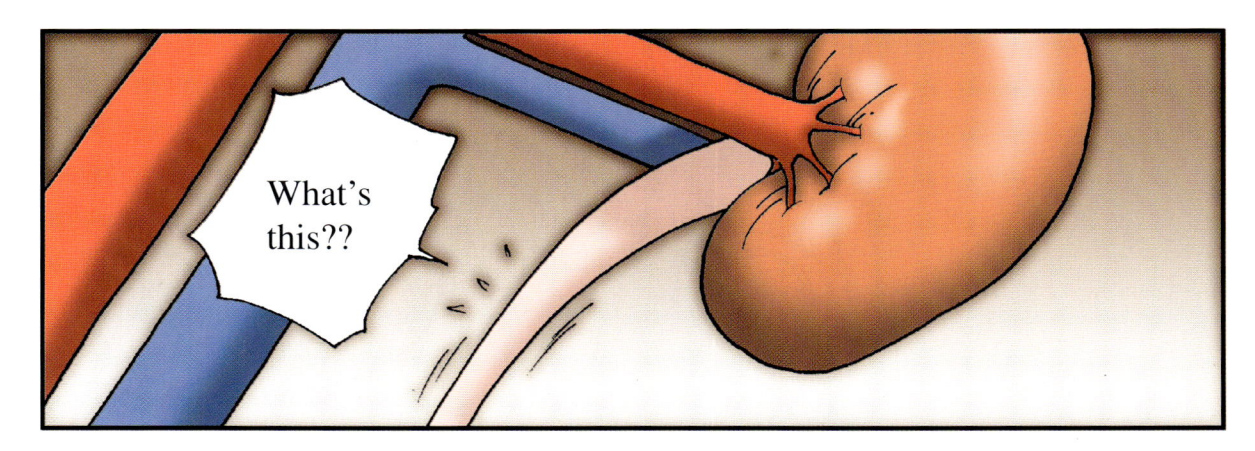

There are complex structures inside the kidneys that separate the waste from the materials the body still needs. Waste materials and extra water are made into urine.

Blood flowing through the many blood vessels in the kidneys reabsorbs the water and nutrients the body will keep.

Ahhh!

What's this??

I think we're falling into the bladder!!
What!?! The bladder!
The bladder is where the urine is collected!!
I know that! Ewww...
More stinky smells?
Ahhhhh!!
BLOOSH

We're in the bladder.
But...it doesn't smell in here.
Actually, urine is odorless. It only smells when it leaves our bodies.
In the air, a chemical reaction occurs that gives urine its smell.
Oh! Thank goodness for that...
Whew!
BEEP BEEP
The radar— It's the Shadow Demon!!
But why is it so loud??

Oh no... Look! This can't be!!

What is it?!

How many Shadow Demons are out there!!?? Maybe the radar is broken...

No... Look...

Oh my gosh!!

The Kidneys

What's going on??!!

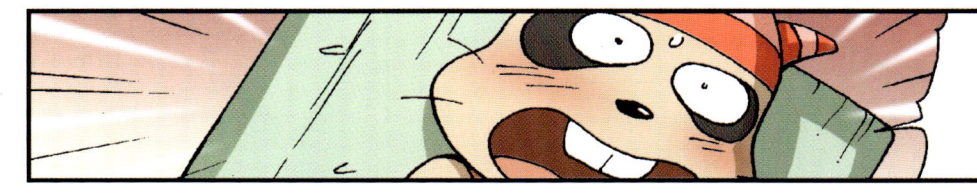

How many Shadow Demons are there?!!

Oh no. We're in big trouble.

This looks like a good place to bury you...

Foolish kids! It's too late for regrets.

I'll turn you into waste!

WOOOSH

The Kidneys 159

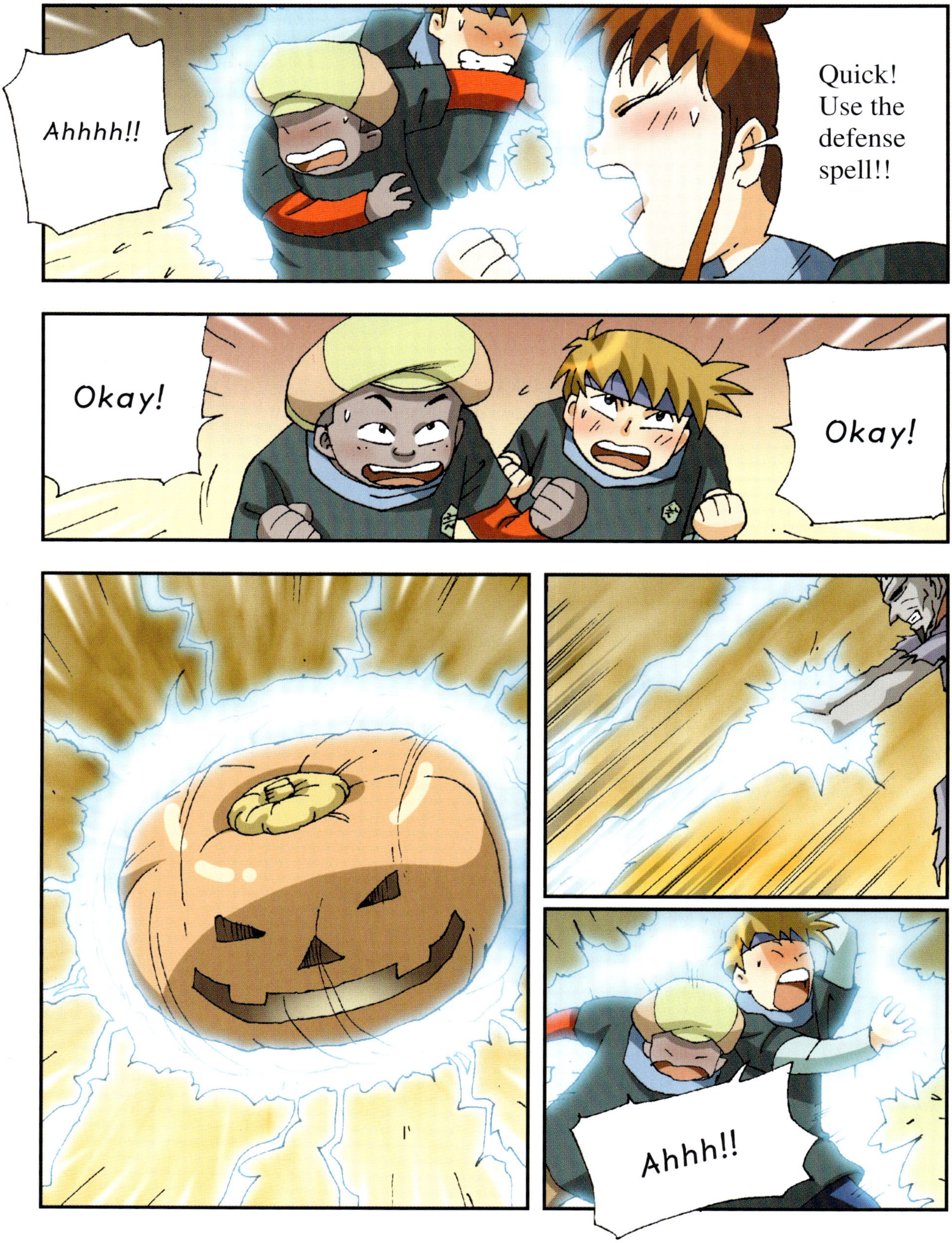
Ahhhh!!
Quick! Use the defense spell!!
Okay!
Okay!
Ahhh!!

We've got to do something.

This shield'll only hold up for so long...

How cute! That'll hold for about thirty seconds.

Ahhhh!!

ACK!!!!

The Kidneys 161

Ken, help! We can't hold out much longer!!

There is only one true demon. The rest are merely illusions...

Really?

The problem is...

...all of his clones have the same power he does! This is bad.

But there is something we can do, right?

Say something, Ken!

....

If only we could find out which one is the real demon.

We have to find the real Shadow Demon?

But how are we going to do that??

Do something! Quick! Before they attack...

That's it!! We'll use mines to blow them up!

The Kidneys 163

Heeheehee!

The magic mines wipe out magic powers, so all the demon clones will disappear!

Take that, Shadow Demon!

What are they up to now?

BANG

BANG

164 A Journey into the Human Body

Those kids...

Fire the net!!!

I'll get you for this!!

We lost him again...
Shoot! I was sure we had him.
Look. We can see where the Shadow Demon is going!!
That's because the mines were filled with a detecting agent...
..and it lasts for days!
The Shadow Demon is making his way toward the brain.
Then that's where we'll go, too. We're coming to get you, Shadow Demon!!
Great! It's our turn to take him by surprise!!

Inferior Vena Cava

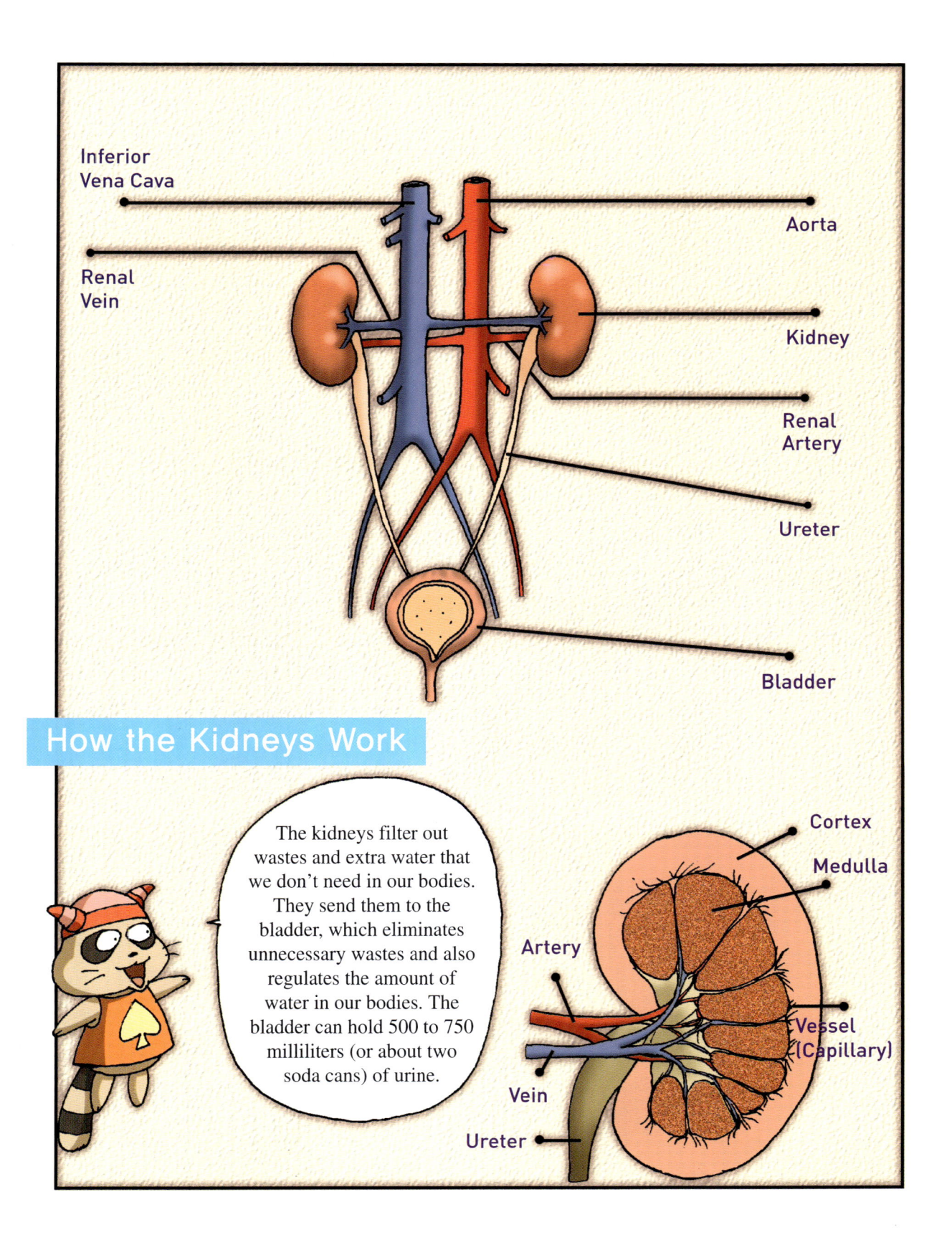

Aorta

Renal Vein

Kidney

Renal Artery

Ureter

Bladder

How the Kidneys Work

The kidneys filter out wastes and extra water that we don't need in our bodies. They send them to the bladder, which eliminates unnecessary wastes and also regulates the amount of water in our bodies. The bladder can hold 500 to 750 milliliters (or about two soda cans) of urine.

Cortex

Medulla

Artery

Vessel (Capillary)

Vein

Ureter

The Kidneys **167**

The Brain

This is the cerebral cortex.

There's still a lot to learn about the brain. Much of it remains a mystery, like outer space.

Well, it does look like a maze.

I heard that the brain is divided into different sections, is that right?

168 A Journey into the Human Body

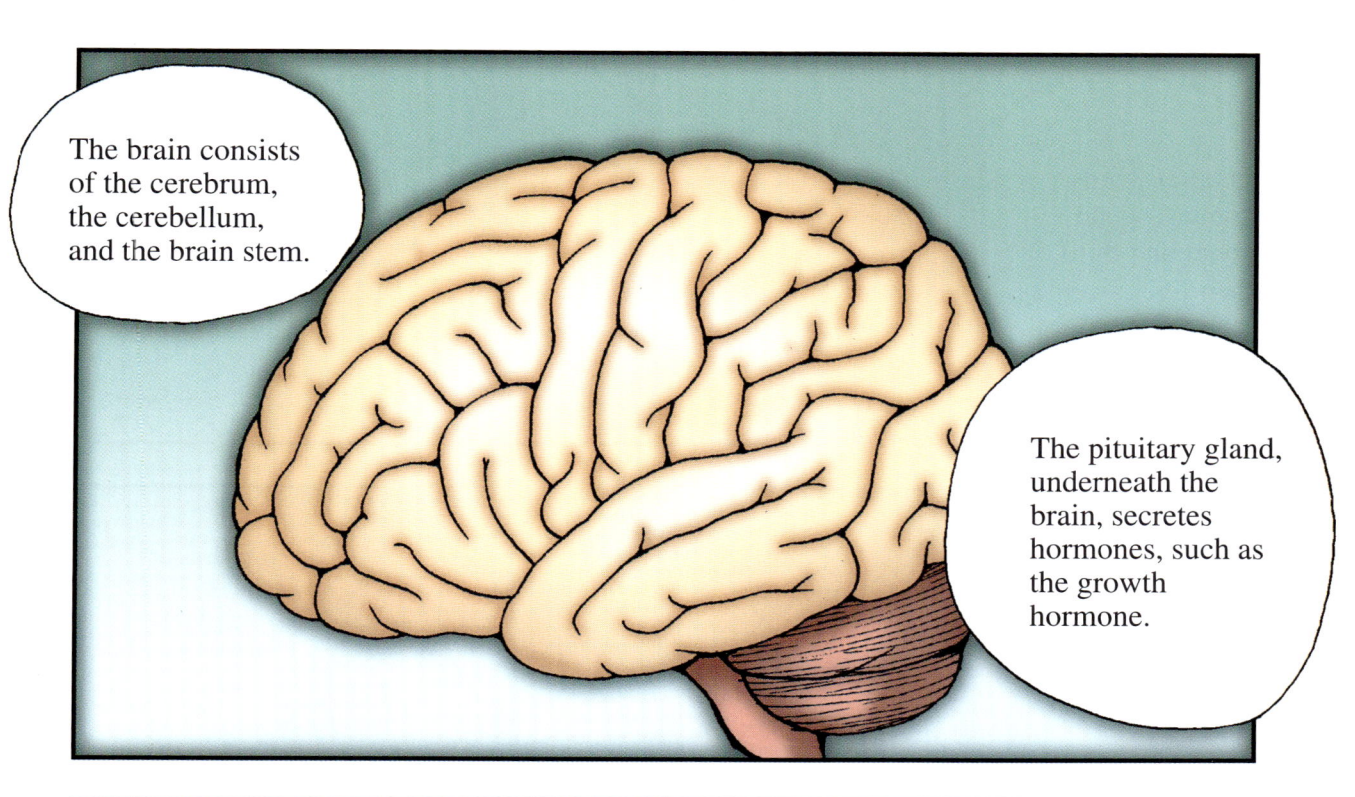

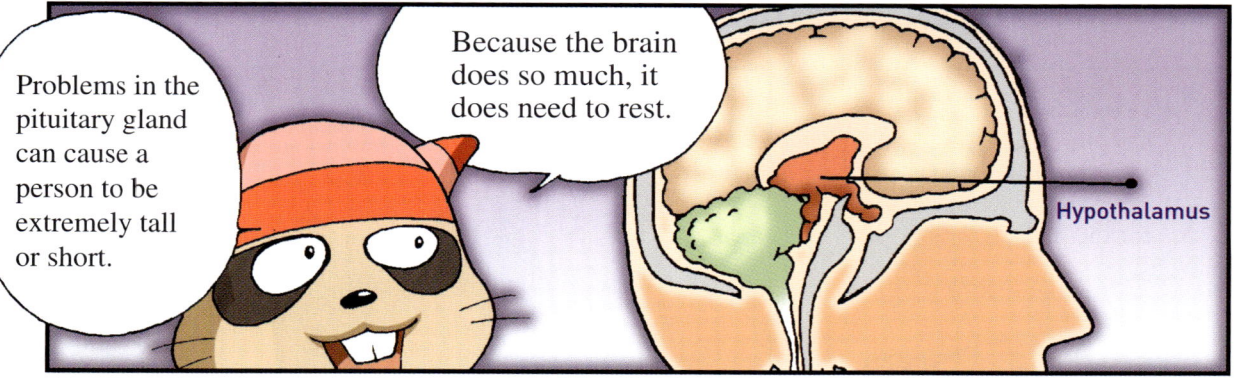

The brain consists of the cerebrum, the cerebellum, and the brain stem.

The pituitary gland, underneath the brain, secretes hormones, such as the growth hormone.

Problems in the pituitary gland can cause a person to be extremely tall or short.

Because the brain does so much, it does need to rest.

Hypothalamus

You're talking about sleep, right?

Right. It is said that humans spend twenty years of their lives sleeping.

Twenty years??!!

In other words, humans spend about one-third of their lives sleeping.
When we sleep, the brain gets a chance to rest and restore its energy. That's why sleep is so important.
Why do people dream?
Dreams are the result of signals that are sent to the brain.
Dreams can last anywhere from five to ten minutes. One person is believed to have dreamt for 150 minutes.
That's nothing! I dream all day!
But the most important function of the brain is learning.

It's thanks to the brain that humans are able to solve hard problems.

Learning is the ability to memorize or remember something. Not even the brightest scientists know how this happens.

They don't know??

Yeah...That's why the brain is still such a mystery.

We're nearly caught up with the Shadow Demon.

BEEP BEEP

I wonder how close we are?

We're really close.

I don't think he's seen us yet.

The Brain 171

Then let's go outside. It's time for the final battle.
Okay!
Don't we need the net?
This is all we need!
The gold hammer!
Yup, it's the Mountain Giant's hammer.
You know how he turns everything to gold? The headmaster gave it to me.
Wow! Cool!

T-that's...!!

Oh my gosh!

Shadow Demon's eggs...

He's trying to hatch several hundred of his eggs in here...

He's been trying to protect his eggs.

We can't let him get away with this.

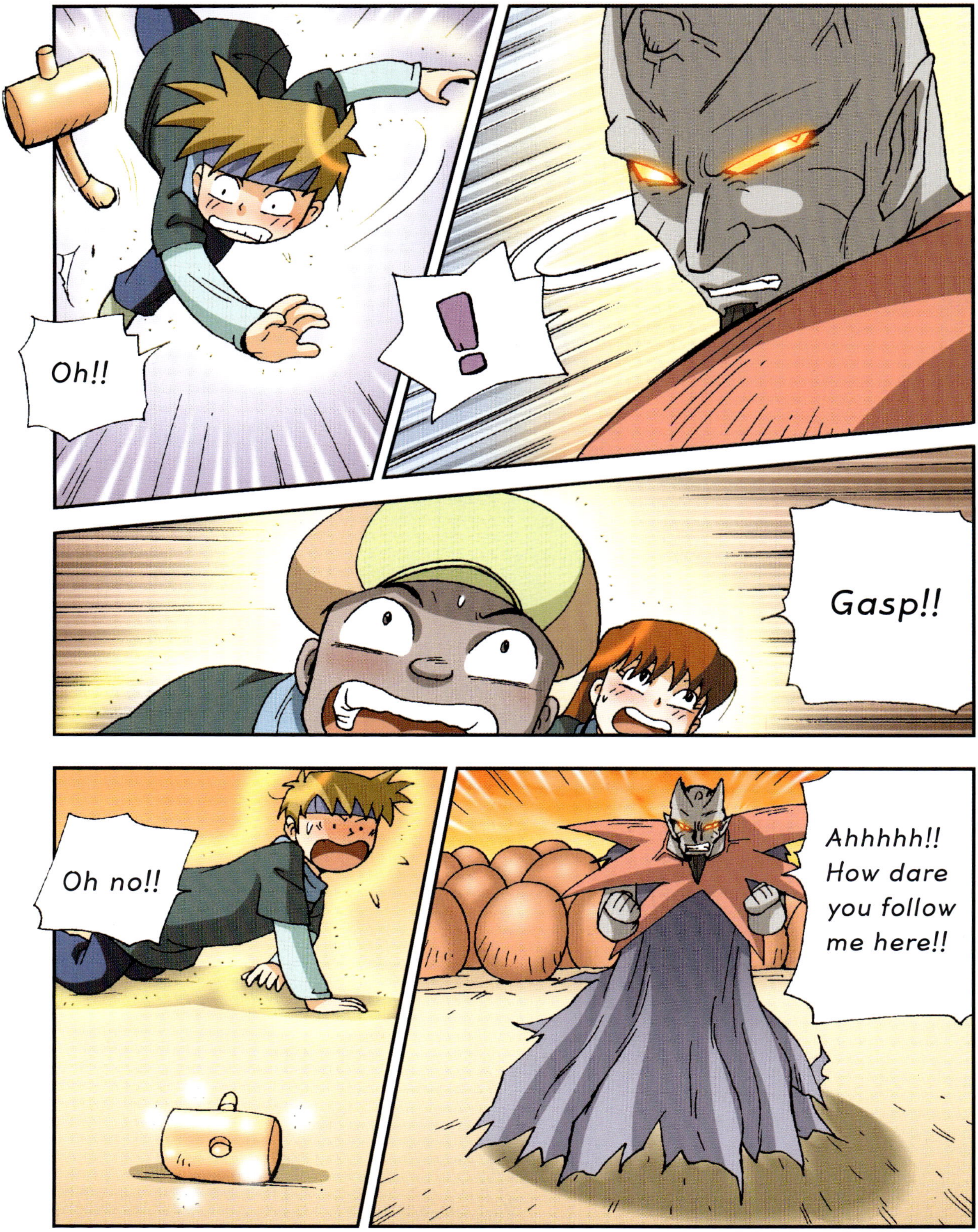
Oh!!
!
Gasp!!
Oh no!!
Ahhhhh!! How dare you follow me here!!

쉬숨어도쓰!!

POP

Hehehe... The Shadow Dragon!

I'll get rid of you pesky kids first before I move on to your friends and Romeo... Then I'll destroy the entire human race!!

The Brain

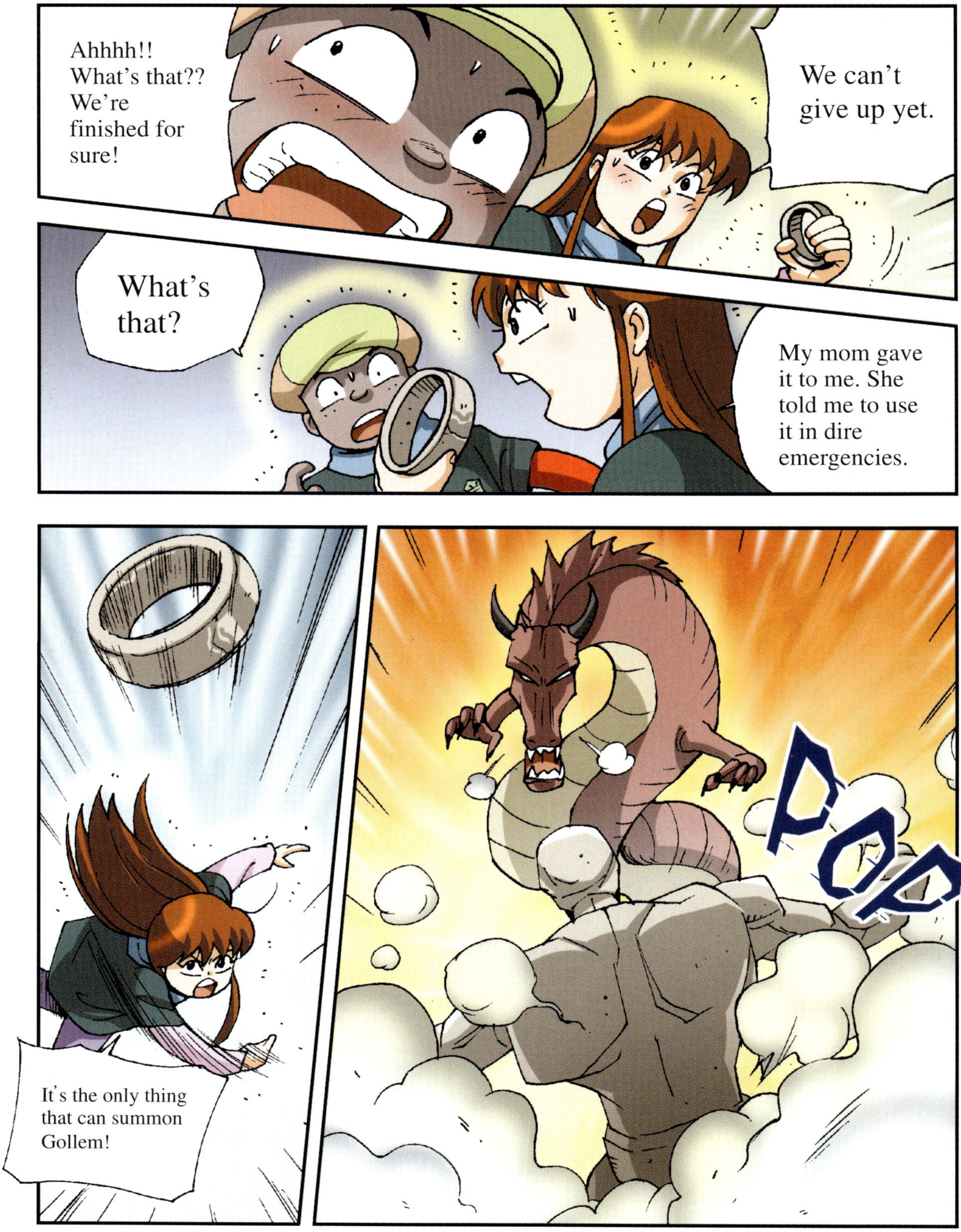
Ahhhh!! What's that?? We're finished for sure!
We can't give up yet.
What's that?
My mom gave it to me. She told me to use it in dire emergencies.
It's the only thing that can summon Gollem!
POP

You're doing a good job, Gollem.

Gollem! Destroy the Shadow Dragon! Now!

Gollem!! Those kids...!!

The Brain 177

Oh no!

We challenge you, Shadow Demon!

Argh... N—no...

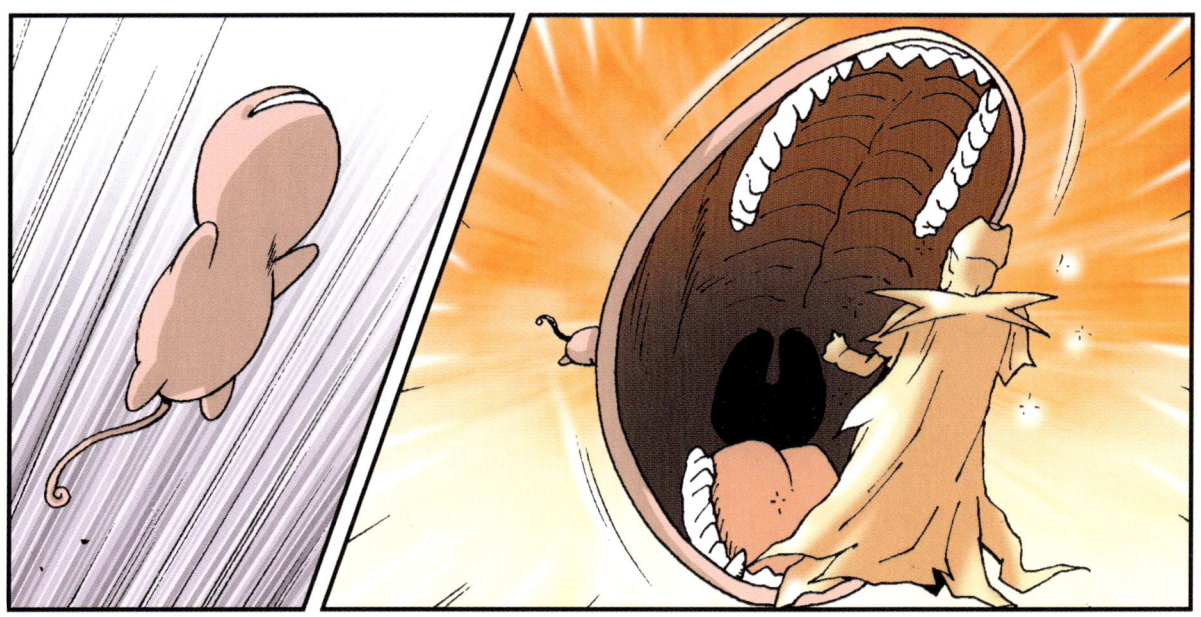

BUMP

Your turn, Colossical!!

The Brain 179

Yayyyyy?!
Hehehe! We finally got him!! Yay!!
We got him!!
We did it! We did it!!
Let's hurry up and get out of here. They'll be waiting for us!
If the demon's not here to blow his magic into them, the eggs'll dissolve into thin air!

The Structure of the Brain

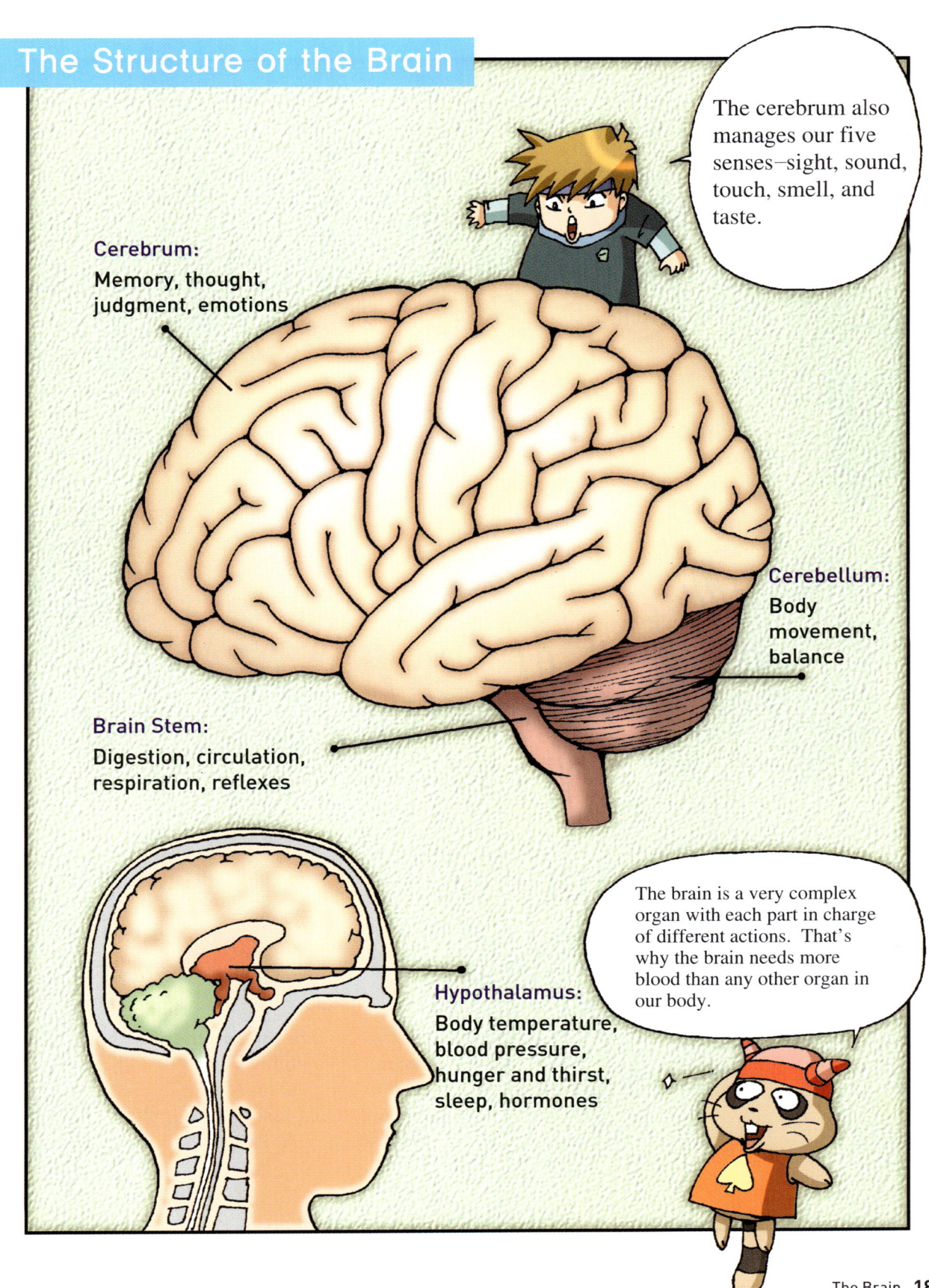

The cerebrum also manages our five senses—sight, sound, touch, smell, and taste.

Cerebrum: Memory, thought, judgment, emotions

Cerebellum: Body movement, balance

Brain Stem: Digestion, circulation, respiration, reflexes

Hypothalamus: Body temperature, blood pressure, hunger and thirst, sleep, hormones

The brain is a very complex organ with each part in charge of different actions. That's why the brain needs more blood than any other organ in our body.

The Brain 181

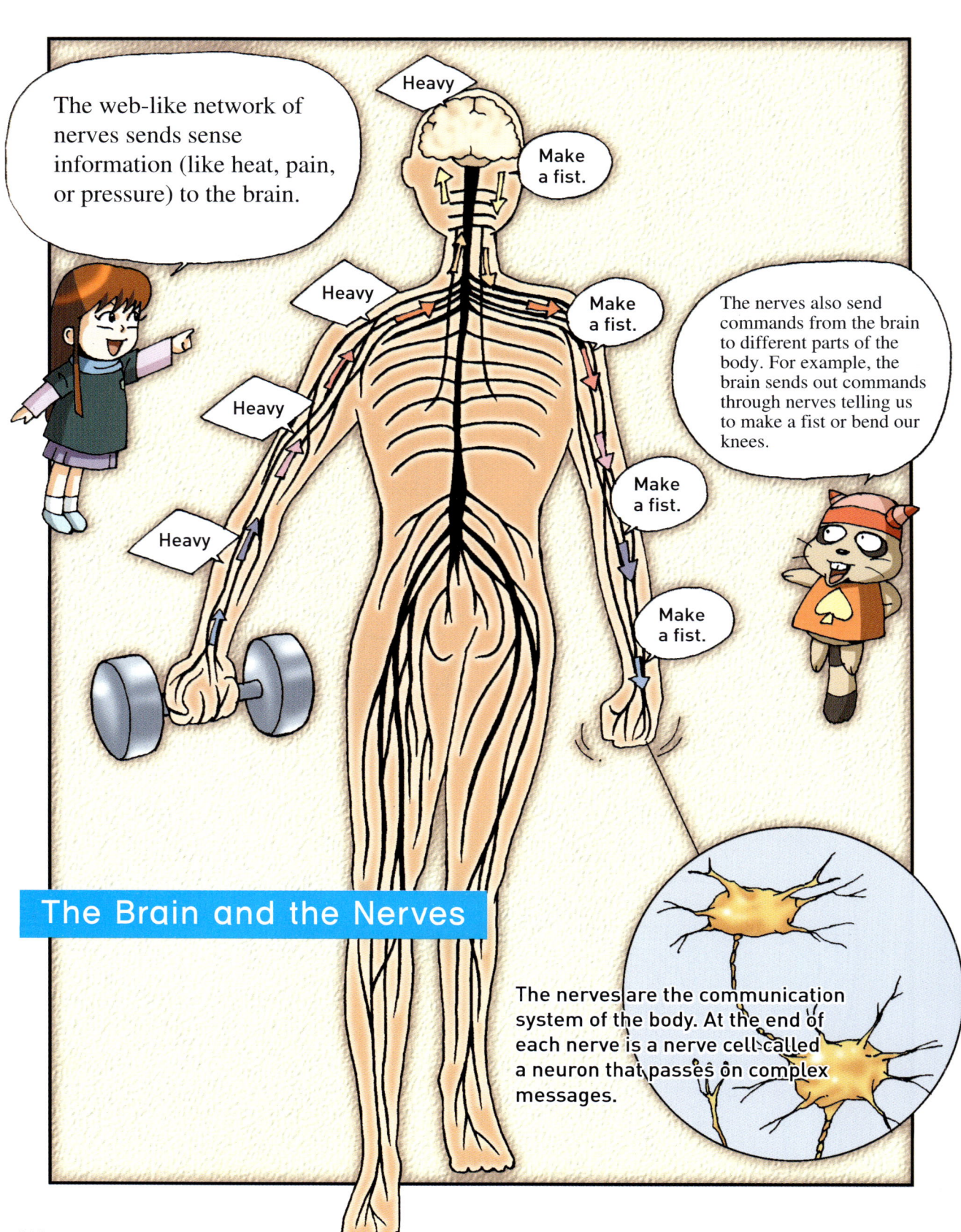

The web-like network of nerves sends sense information (like heat, pain, or pressure) to the brain.

Heavy
Make a fist.
Heavy
Make a fist.
Heavy
Make a fist.
Heavy
Make a fist.
Heavy
Make a fist.

The nerves also send commands from the brain to different parts of the body. For example, the brain sends out commands through nerves telling us to make a fist or bend our knees.

The Brain and the Nerves

The nerves are the communication system of the body. At the end of each nerve is a nerve cell called a neuron that passes on complex messages.

Going Home

Here. This is the Goblin black box that Colossical had when he ate the Shadow Demon.

You did well!!

Sunny, Yuna, and Joon— You have brought honor to our school.

I am very proud of you.

I am also proud of these kids, Mr. Romeo.

You are our heroes.

Right!

Hmmm...

Huh?? Are we going to be punished?

Yes, but they still broke the rules.

Of course. If you hadn't broken the rules in the first place, none of this would've happened.

That's not fair! We almost died!

I'm sorry, but the superintendent is in charge of the dorms.

Sunny. Joon. Yuna...

"From now until the day you graduate, I will allow you to share a special three-bedroom suite."

"What?"

"Huh? A special suite?!"

"Yaayy!"

"Hahahaha!!"

"Waaahoooo!!"

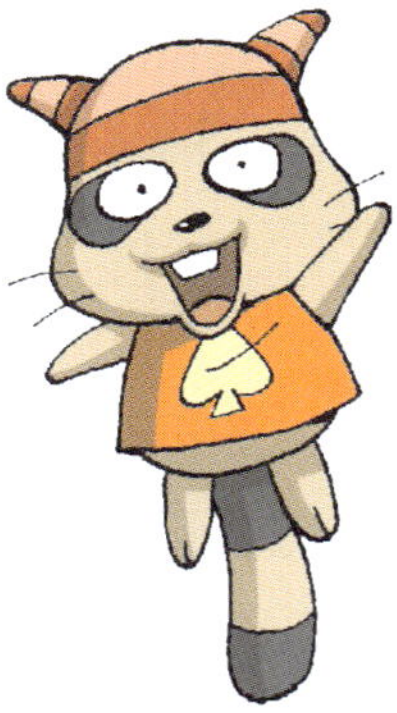

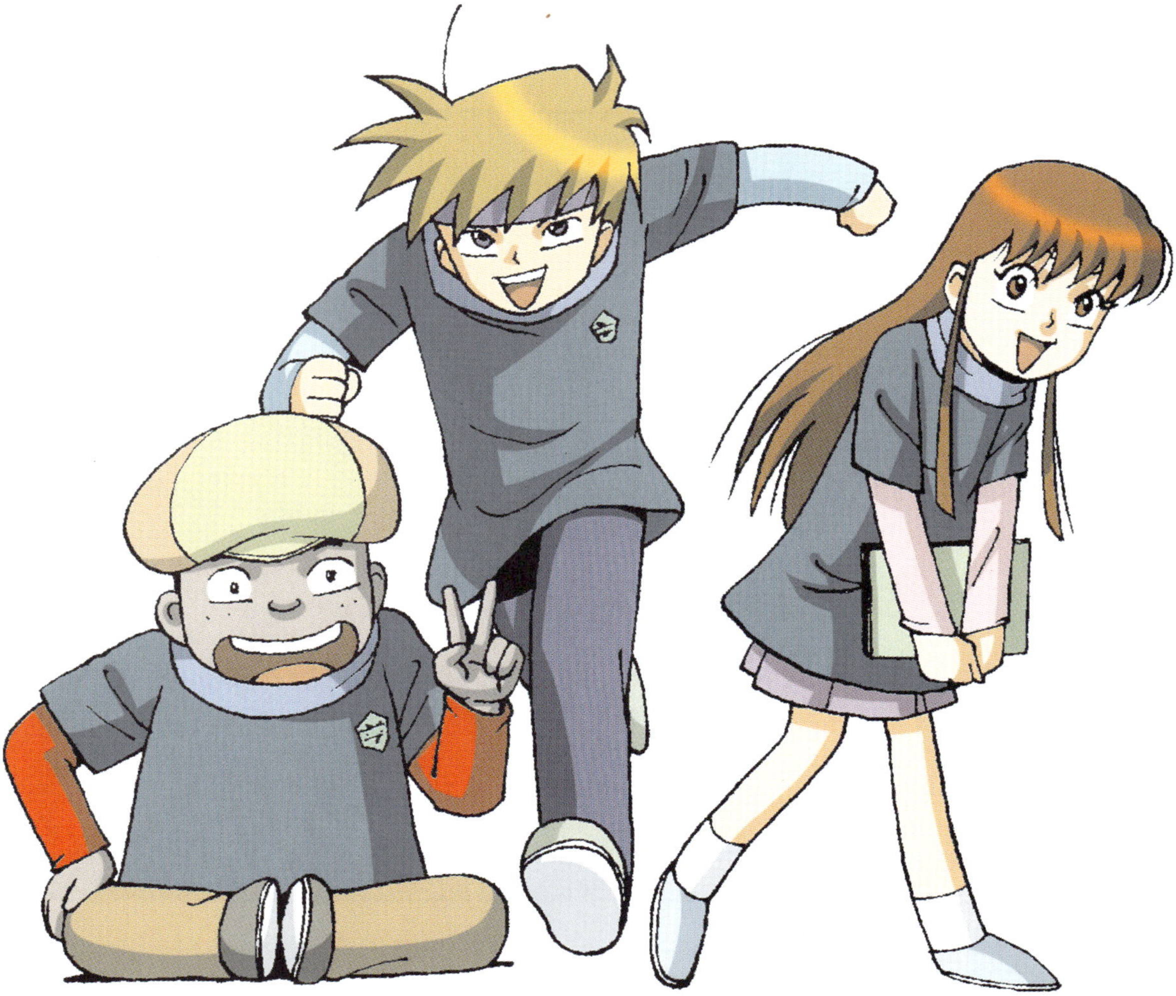

Memo

Memo